# OUTSTANDING LEADERSHIP

# OUTSTANDING LEADERSHIP

## STAN TOLER

**HARVEST HOUSE PUBLISHERS**
EUGENE, OREGON

*Cover by Dugan Design Group*

*Cover illustrations © iStock / seamartini, kristina-s*

Published in association with Meadow's Edge Group

**OUTSTANDING LEADERSHIP**

Copyright © 2016 by Stan Toler
Published by Harvest House Publishers
Eugene, Oregon 97402
www.harvesthousepublishers.com

ISBN 978-0-7369-6823-2
ISBN 978-0-7369-6824-9 (eBook)

**Printed in China**

16 17 18 19 20 21 22 23 24 / RDS-JH / 10 9 8 7 6 5 4 3 2 1

# Contents

# Introduction

*Aspiring leaders acknowledge that the
achievement of others offers a key to
unlocking their own excellence.*

once read about a freight train that traveled 70 miles
through northwest Ohio at speeds close to 50 miles per
hour *by itself*!

As the train was being assembled, the braking system
failed, and it suddenly took off. Near Kenton, the train slowed
to about 10 miles per hour. A railroad employee started running alongside the runaway train, grabbed a railing on the die-
sel, and jumped on board, finally bringing the 47-car train to
a stop.[1]

There are times when leadership is a lot like trying to stop a
runaway train. An organization can move toward its perceived
destination under its own power as its leader runs alongside,
frustrated and out of breath. At other times, the organizational
train never leaves the station. The machinery is in place and
the route is mapped, but nothing is moving.

Leadership isn't about moving machinery; it's about

moving people in a preferred direction toward a destination born out of vision.

Becky Hammon is a product of leadership that moves people. She was named as the first full-time female assistant coach in the National Basketball Association.

A star basketball player at Colorado State, Becky was always on a fast track to all-American status. What motivated her to greatness? In part, it was the affirmation of one leader, an assistant coach on the Colorado team.

The coach kept telling her she would do great things. Hammon reflects, "When she started speaking all that, she started planting seeds. 'Yeah, maybe. Maybe I could do that if I worked really hard.' You have those people speaking really good things in your life and it grows and produces fruit later on." The San Antonio Spurs assistant emphasized, "Somebody had to initially plant those good seeds."[2]

---

*Leadership isn't about moving machinery; it's about moving people in a preferred direction toward a destination born out of vision.*

---

This is a book about planting seeds, about relating to people and motivating them to be all-stars in your organization.

*Outstanding Leadership* focuses on people, not just plans and programs. It is born out of my 40-plus years of experiences as an executive leader of a denomination, a pastor of churches that grew from small or midsize constituencies into large churches, and a teacher of seminars on personal and organizational growth that have helped more than a million attendees sharpen and expand their leadership skills.

In a more important sense, it is a personal letter to you, right where you are or where you hope to be on your leadership journey. I will help you grow in ten leadership areas as you learn how to...

- define an organizational vision
- develop a vision plan
- cast an inspiring vision to your constituency
- test your organizational vision for quality
- identify and use your leadership and vision skills
- set coaching objectives
- overcome leadership challenges
- communicate effectively with your team
- build winning relationships
- develop transformational leadership

In addition, I've provided valuable sidebar information, including tips from leaders of major corporations and organizations. (URLs are in the endnotes—I think you will find them to be great resources for further study on relational and motivational leadership.)

You may have a brilliant idea or product, a well-crafted vision plan to capture its uniqueness, and a highly organized vision-casting team to communicate it, but if you don't have constituent or customer buy-in, your idea will probably gather dust on a shelf. I want to show you how to make it come alive, how to *sell* your vision plan through your team to your public, including your stakeholders.

Leadership never has an arrival date. It's a never-ending journey filled with the joy of developing people, casting visions, and launching projects that will add value to the lives of others.

*Mine has been a journey of faith.* My personal relationship with God has given me the opportunity to serve him in more than 90 countries of the world with some of his top-level team members.

*Mine has been a journey of relationships.* Along the way, I have been inspired and challenged by the leadership of others. They served as my teachers and helped to shape my thoughts on working with people and building relationships. And of course, my family and friends have affirmed and encouraged me in an awesome and loving way.

*Mine has been a journey of love.* I love what I do! To think that a boy from the poorest town in America could have an international network that includes people from nearly all cultures and economic groups is humbling and beyond anything I could have dreamed.

I hope and pray that your own leadership will be enriched by *Outstanding Leadership* and that you will lead with a strong emphasis on mentoring next-generation leaders.

# Part 1

# Leadership That Motivates

Chapter 1

# Defining Your Vision

*Leaders not only have an eye on the*
*horizon, they can see just beyond it.*

everal years ago, the host of an event where I was speaking
sent word that he wouldn't be able to meet me at the airport. When I asked how to find the person who would
be driving me to the event, the host replied, "Just look for
someone who looks like they're looking for you." If you've
spent much time in the baggage claim area of a major airport,
you know that would include almost everybody.

After several anxious minutes—and much looking for
someone who looked like they might be looking for me—I
spotted a man holding up a cardboard sign that read, "Dr.
Stand Taller." Relieved to have found my driver, I walked
toward him and said, "I'm trying! Honest, I'm trying!"

People need leaders who have a vision that relates to them
and motivates them to action. They are looking for you, looking for leaders who will "stand taller." They want leaders
with tall dreams and ambitions for themselves and for the

organizations they lead. They want leaders with a vision that connects with people and draws them in.

## Vision and People

An effective vision is people-driven. It is defined and distributed with *people* in mind—people who will have a part in the process. Allyson Willoughby, in a *Leadership Now* article on creating a workplace employees love, said, "It's important that employees...feel part of the decision-making process...Having their voice heard during these discussions can go a long way when it comes to employee satisfaction."[1]

A 1972 advertisement for Greyhound Lines said, "When you deal in basic needs, you're always needed." More recently, Greyhound CEO Dave Leach said, "[We're] changing from an operational-focus organization to a customer- and employee-focused organization."[2]

---

### Five Traits That Most "Employers of Choice" Have in Common

1. People matter.

2. Employees feel heard.

3. People are empowered to grow.

4. Leaders are strong.

5. Employees are appreciated.[3]

---

Author Dale Galloway defined vision as "the ability, or the God-given gift, to see those things that are not as becoming a reality."[4] Martin Luther King Jr. embodied this definition in his last speech, "I've Been to the Mountaintop"—a prophetic look toward a better time and the Promised Land.

Vision is an organization's perceived direction based on its ideas and ideals. Whether it is framed in an organization's statement of vision or mission, it is a dream extended by the leaders that grasps the hearts and minds of core followers. Vision has a simple framework.

- It usually begins with a person or group's perceived solution to a common problem or need.

- It takes shape based on perceived steps that will propel a solution.

- It resides in the parameters of opportunity, skills, time, finances, and staffing.

- It lives and grows with buy-in from people who are convinced that they (and others) will be affected in a positive and helpful way.

Kenneth Labich offered this reminder of the power of a clear vision:

> Don't underestimate the power of a vision. McDonald's founder, Ray Kroc, pictured his empire long before it existed, and he saw how to get it there. He invented the company

motto—"Quality, service, cleanliness and value"—and kept repeating it to employees for the rest of his life. [5]

## Vision and Direction

The classic story of the politician giving a rousing speech against the evils of society illustrates the importance of a relational vision. "I pledge to rid the world of ageism, sexism, despotism, racism, and nepotism!" he exclaimed.

The crowd was electrified, and soon the applause was deafening. But when it died down, an elderly gentleman shouted out, "Good luck, mister! I've been trying to get rid of *rheumatism* for the last ten years!"

A vision that doesn't affect people where they live is a lot like a fake Christmas tree—it has the look and feel of the real thing, but it just doesn't smell right. A vision that relates provides team members and constituents with a cause and an accompanying cure—based on a need-answering, concise direction and destination.

A people-driven vision must also include...

definite places,
definite times, and
tangible results.

## Vision and Practice

In his book *Coach Wooden: The 7 Principles That Shaped His Life and Will Change Yours*, Pat Williams shares the story of the legendary John Wooden. He relates that Wooden's life and career were shaped by a piece of paper handed to him at his graduation by his beloved father. It had a poem on one side and "Seven Rules for Living" on the other. That paper, along with a two-dollar bill, was all Joshua Wooden could afford to give his son, but the principles on the reverse side shaped the life of the coach—and every player he taught during his stellar career.

Many of the athletes he coached—whose pictures hang in basketball's Hall of Fame or who have excelled in business, education, or leadership—carry a copy of those principles to this day, including Williams.

1. Be true to yourself.

2. Help others.

3. Make each day your masterpiece.

4. Drink deeply from good books, especially the Bible.

5. Make friendship a fine art.

6. Build a shelter against a rainy day by the life you live.

7. Pray for guidance and counsel, and give thanks for your blessings each day. [6]

Hardly the content of philosophy, business, or management textbooks in most colleges or universities today, those seven down-home sentences motivated Coach Wooden and his team members to create one of the winningest basketball organizations in history.

---

*A vision that relates provides team members and constituents with a cause and an accompanying cure—based on a need-answering, concise direction and destination.*

---

A prominent religious leader was asked how his bestselling pamphlet on discovering a personal faith should be shared with intellectuals. He answered, "Just read slower." Practical always trumps theoretical.

A vision must be practical. It must result in reasonable, people-focused goals and objectives. If people can't relate to the vision, it is likely irrelevant. Conversely, if a vision is definitive and easy to relate to, it gains relevance and buy-in as it is developed and distributed. As someone once said, "Motivate people to buy into and live the wisdom."

If you will have a vision that motivates and relates, you must...

- envision it

- think it through

- write it out in its simplest, yet most detailed form

- be able to explain its details in a simple way

- illustrate its beginning, middle, and ending

And then watch its tiny seed blossom in excellent team efforts, especially in those team members whose input will help to flesh it out and in the hearts of customers or constituents.

## Vision and Motivation

A vision should be inspirational! Motivation is directly linked to personalization—it inspires people to act and respond. Carl Jung said, "Your vision will become clear only when you look into your own heart. Who looks outside, dreams; who looks inside, awakes." When a plan or program or product personally affects us, we have an immediate stake in it.

### Leadership Is About Emotion

Great leaders...

- read people's (often unstated, sometimes unconscious) needs and desires

- welcome new knowledge and fresh input (even if challenging)

- know that what worked in one situation may be useless in another

- know that talented people don't need or want hovering managers

- have a reputation for honesty

- treat everyone with a basic level of respect

- communicate the organization's strategies, goals, and challenges

- find out what employees' career goals are and help them reach them[7]

A vision is birthed in the mind and heart. It is a dynamic, fire-breathing dream of something that has never been done or needs to be done to increase the quality of life. The visionary leader is struck with a solution that will make things better. In the short term, it is the tiger on the loose. It roams or sits where it pleases. In the long term, it is the tiger that has been housebroken. It is trained and on a leash.

The motivation matures. It is assigned a practical direction. Those who surround it become acquainted with it and, we hope, identify with it. In fact, the vision is effective only as long as people identify with it. Leaders who motivate and relate hold the leash on the tiger. Where they lead the vision—and how people relate to it—will depend on how it is introduced.

*Where there is no vision, the people perish.*

**PROVERBS 29:18**

## Vision and Values

Leaders hold the keys to the "values gate." Like it or not, the ethical nature of an organization is under their watch. Former president George H.W. Bush gave some practical, value-laden advice to such leaders:

> First, no matter how hard-fought the issue, never get personal...
>
> Second, do your homework. You can't lead without knowing what you are talking about...
>
> Third, the American legislative process is one of give and take. Use your power as a leader to persuade, not intimidate...
>
> Fouth, be considerate of the needs of your colleagues, even if they're at the bottom of the totem pole. [8]

Leaders need all the advice they can get—and sometimes get more than they want! But as captain of the organizational vessel, you are responsible to...

- chart the course,
- recruit and motivate the crew,
- secure the cargo, and
- keep the vessel on course till it reaches the destination.

You are also responsible to keep it up to code, to make sure it passes moral inspection by its constituents. The values of your "vessel" are most often a reflection of your own personal values. So great caution should be taken to make sure your organization stands tall in its community. How?

*1. Stay on track.* More than likely you have taken time to construct a statement of purpose—documenting the "whats, whys, and wherefores" of your organization. Your next important task will be to keep your organization and its products or services on track.

*2. Don't advertise something you can't deliver.* The integrity of many organizations has been tarnished by $100 ads for $10 programs! If you can't deliver the best, biggest, or most spectacular output on the face of the earth, don't promise that you can.

*3. Treat staff with respect.* As someone once said, "You're known not only by the company you keep but also by how you keep your company." Your encouragement, compassion, training, and support for your staff will soon be well known in your community. (They'll also hear about staff abuse in a hurry!)

*4. Be open about plans and programs.* Some leaders act as if they're conducting an undercover operation. A lack of publicity about organizational programs or plans is a surefire integrity killer.

A friend of mine was once invited to be a staff member of a religious organization. When he arrived to begin his responsibilities, he soon discovered that his superior had neglected to tell anyone in the organization about the hire—including the governing board. A tsunami of embarrassment soon covered all hopes of my friend's staff position. And the leader in charge of the covert operation lost his parking space.

*5. Keep the financial books open.* Stakeholders want to be informed when the cash flows and when it ebbs. One of the most important documents that an organization can publish is its financial report. Workhorses are skittish.

*6. Protect the integrity of the workers.* When new hires walk in the door of your organization, you are responsible for more than their health benefits and payroll. You are responsible to provide a safe environment.

Safety awareness includes more than passing out hard hats. It also includes providing an environment where staff members know they won't suffer any kind of harassment, where they feel accepted and appreciated, and where they are free to contribute to the organization's mission with excellence.

*7. Focus on the main thing.* Your greatest challenge will probably be to keep the organizational oars in the water, paddling in the direction of its mission. Along the way, you'll be tempted to take side trips or look for shortcuts. Your institution's integrity will also be known by its focus. Can it avoid expensive or faddish mission add-ons? That's up to you. When all else fails, stay the course.

War hero and former president of the United States Dwight D. Eisenhower said, "If a man's associates find him guilty of phoniness, if they find that he lacks forthright integrity, he will fail. His teachings and actions must square with each other. The first great need, therefore, is integrity and high purpose."[9]

A police officer once backed his cruiser into the alley beside the bank in a small town. He needed one more ticket to impress the new police chief.

Suddenly he spotted one of the town's senior citizens exiting from the only restaurant in town, a Kentucky Fried Chicken franchise connected to a corner convenience store. Grandpa climbed into the borrowed car—his grandson's new Mustang. But he was so impressed with the car that he forgot the bucket of chicken he had set on the roof before he climbed in.

Grandpa drove down Main Street a bit too fast and right through the town's only stop sign.

"This is my chance," the rookie officer thought as he switched on the flashing lights and pulsing siren.

Grandpa slowly pulled over. The police officer briskly walked to the driver's side, took the bucket of chicken from the roof, and held it to the window for Grandpa to see.

Unfazed, Grandpa rolled down the window and said with a kindly smile, "No thanks, son. I bought a bucket for myself."

Both were doing their jobs—the officer was protecting the law, and the grandpa was protecting his reputation as a generous and upstanding citizen of the community.

Do your job to the best of your ability and foster the best in others. This may be your best chance to define a world-changing vision, one that will make the world better for grandpas, police officers, and everyone else in your community.

In the next chapter, we'll look at the process of manufacturing the vision.

Chapter 2

# Developing a Vision Plan

*Leaders know the journey is made of individual
steps, each firmly planted in uncharted territory.*

A history professor commented on Christopher Columbus's discovery of America. He pointed out three significant aspects of the trip:

One, before Columbus departed, he didn't have
a clue where he was going.

Two, when he arrived, he didn't have a clue
where he was.

And three, when he got ready to leave, he didn't
have a clue how to get back home.

An economics major spoke up from the back of the room.
"And four, he didn't have a clue how he was going to pay back
that loan to the government!"

Strategic planning is the process of clarifying a direction
for the future (a vision plan) and formulating specific, measurable actions that will move the organization toward that vision.

It is a must process for every organization that seeks to make its mark in today's culture.

In my book *Stan Toler's Practical Guide to Leading Staff*, I talk about how a vision affects priorities.

> When you declare your vision, it becomes a matter of record. Your vision affects the goals you want to reach, the records you want to break, and the finish lines you want to cross. A challenging goal tends to motivate us. First we make the goal; then the goal makes us as it pulls us toward it.[1]

Michael Dell, founder of Dell Computer, reflected on the vision of his company in an interview with Jon Swartz for *USA Today*.

> "The world got enamored with smartphones and tablets," Dell says. "But what's interesting is those devices don't do everything that needs to be done. Three-D printing, virtual-reality computing, robotics are all controlled by PCs. Productivity is grounded in the PC.
>
> "Where does the computing power come from?" Dell says, leaning forward. "How would you run *USA Today* without PCs? Run a hospital without PCs?

"People don't want products, they want solutions," Dell says.[2]

*People want solutions.* The core principle of a developing vision plan is its impact on people's needs. Organizations built solely on steel and plastic and a rigid corporate infrastructure will slowly drift into the sunset unless they have a mindset of "customer first" and "opinion matters."

What are the essentials of a vision plan?

## A Vision Plan Is Based on Your Story

Watch how quickly visitors to a corporate headquarters migrate to the pictures on the wall. Whether displayed in the building's atrium or on the walls of its hallways or conference rooms, the pictures are people magnets. They love to see the past and present of an organization visualized.

Paul Argenti and Janis Forman give valuable storytelling advice in their book *The Power of Corporate Communications: Crafting the Voice and Image of Your Business.*

> The story can be told through official mission statements, declarations of identity, and any other means of communication with all constituencies. In particular, the main sources that external constituencies will rely on for information about your company and the story you are telling include articles in publications, television ads, discussions about the company

with other people (for example, family, friends, and colleagues), and direct interaction with company employees. [3]

Notice the emphases—"constituencies," "people," "direct interaction with company employees." The organizational story is people-friendly.

I love the story of the elderly lady who was standing in a long line at the post office. When a postal worker approached her and suggested that she might try the self-service kiosk nearby, the lady pointed to the postal worker at the desk in front of the line. "No thanks," she said. "I've been coming to this post office for 20 years, and that fella up there at the desk always asks about my rheumatism."

If the lady in line were to write the story of that USPS branch, she would emphasize its personalized service. Who is telling your organization's story? What product or service have you produced that has had a life-changing impact on them? Get their stories and include them in yours.

## What an Organization's Story Should Include

- What vision motivated its founding?

- What convictions served as its roots?

- What turning points determined its direction?

- Who were the leaders who left special imprints on its development?

- Are there skeletons in the closet that won't go away?

- How does its history impact your leadership?[4]

## A Vision Plan Begins with Leadership

The vision apple never falls far from the leadership tree.

Noted businessman and author Max De Pree said, "The first responsibility of a leader is to define reality."[5] You are the captain that keeps the vision on course. Your values serve as its vessel, your ideas are its mapping points, and your inspiration is the wind in its sails. So you must know where you are heading.

- Identify the problems and solutions.

- Inventory the staffing and funding issues.

- Seek buy-in from your constituencies.

- Formulate preliminary plans for the launch.

My friend John C. Maxwell famously said, "A leader is one who knows the way, goes the way, and shows the way."

A classic story describes the urgency of leadership. Its origin is unknown, but its message is always relevant.

Every morning in Africa, a gazelle wakes up. It knows it must run faster than the fastest lion, or it will be eaten.

Every morning in Africa, a lion wakes up. It knows it must outrun the slowest gazelle, or it will starve to death.

It doesn't matter whether you are a lion or a gazelle. When the sun comes up, you better start running.

## A Vision Plan Focuses on the Needs of Others

Author and speaker Nancy Ortberg told of a favorite scene in the movie *Seabiscuit*. The horse's regular jockey had been in an accident and was hospitalized, so another jockey was recruited to take his place in an important race. The new jockey sat by the hospital bed of the rider who was familiar with the racehorse, noting tips that would help his ride.

The injured man told him that if Seabiscuit was behind, he should try to bring him alongside another horse that had "fire in his eye." He explained that Seabiscuit would respond to the look in the horse's eye and would take off—and win the race. [6]

People motivate people. A vision plan that doesn't put fire in the eyes of others will not inspire buy-in.

- What is the main theme of the plan?
- What felt need does the plan address?

- What overall improvement does the plan offer?
- What is the plan's "hook" that will draw others to it?

Another question: Who will ultimately benefit from the plan? Pat Williams said one of the things that made Coach John Wooden so successful was his resolve to help others. "Some people help others as a way of manipulating them...But Coach focuses on helping people who cannot pay him back."[7]

---

*A vision plan that doesn't plant fire in the eyes of others will not inspire buy-in.*

---

Nelson Mandela once defined the leader's responsibility to meet the needs of others.

> What counts in life is not the mere fact that we have lived. It is the difference we have made in the lives of others that will determine the significance of the life we lead.[8]

## A Vision Plan Includes Missional Priorities

What are the die-for principles of your organization? That, of course, is built into your mission statement. It is the fundamental and nonnegotiable stuff that answers the basic questions:

Who are we?
What do we do?

Where are we going?

How and when will we get there?

In the classic Sherlock Holmes novel *Scandal in Bohemia*, Watson is pressed into service to witness Holmes's marriage. In a typically twisted turn of events, the newly married couple drives off from the cathedral site of their marriage of convenience in different carriages. Watson's observations of the events describe many organizations: "They drove away in different directions, and I went off to make my own arrangements."

A vision without a firm philosophical direction is shallow at best. It can be multidimensional, but it weakens if it is multidirectional.

### John C. Maxwell's Vision Questions

- Look within you—what do you feel?

- Look behind you—what have you learned?

- Look around you—what is happening to others?

- Look ahead of you—what is the big picture?

- Look above you—what does God expect of you?

- Look beside you—what resources are available to you?[9]

Jim Collins and Morten T. Hansen wrote, "The factors that determine whether or not a company becomes truly great, even in a chaotic and uncertain world, lie largely with the hands of its people. It is not mainly a matter of what happens to them but a matter of what they create, what they do, and how well they do it."[10]

Along the development path, you may find a few naysayers hiding in the bushes. Their opinions may be based on evidence, but sometimes it will be more circumstantial than factual. In fact, they may try to sidetrack you in the development process.

Daniel Webster gave an opinion during his 1878 congressional speech on adding territories to the United States. "I cannot conceive of anything more ridiculous, more absurd, and more affrontive to all sober judgment than the cry that we are profiting by the acquisition of New Mexico and California. I hold that they are not worth a dollar!"[11]

The territories were added. And time has proved the worth of the venture—and proved that not all advice or opinions are spot-on.

How do you cast the vision? We'll discover some important steps in the next chapter.

## Chapter 3

# Casting a Vision

*Leaders are in the people business. Their primary
function is not to buy, sell, analyze, or ply a
trade. It is to understand and work with people.*

A man once called a nonprofit organization and asked
for the head hog.

The receptionist was flabbergasted by his lack of
respect and answered, "We don't have a head hog in this organization. If you mean you would like to speak to our CEO, Mr.
Alexander, I can connect you to his office."

The caller replied, "Well, whatever. I've got a court order to
give you folks a million-dollar donation on behalf of my Uncle
Ned, who croaked last week."

"Croaked?" the receptionist said, "You mean he passed?"

"Yep...bought the farm...checked out of the big Walmart
line of life. He was my rich uncle, but he had a heart of gold,
and wanted to me to share a few nuggets with your organization.
So if you folk are interested in a mil', get me to the head hog."

The receptionist had an immediate attitude change. She

said, "Oh, in that case, please hold while I get ol' Porky on the line."

Every organization has an obligation to its constituency—extended or immediate. Its vision is about them, whatever their background. The leader's duty is to give them a promising future for their investment.

Fourteen leaders were asked to share their best leadership advice. *Business News Daily* assistant editor Nicole Fallon recorded their answers. Cameron Herold, coach, author, and founder of BackPocket COO, offered this advice:

> Lean out into the future. Pretend you go in a time machine, three years out. Write down in three to four pages exactly what your company looks like. Describe every aspect of your company at that time. That's your "painted picture." Then hand that vivid description to your team. Now that they can see what you can see, they can figure out how to make it happen.[1]

How will you give form to your vision? In Herold's words, hand it your team.

## Create a Vision Team

A vision team may be an appointed, four- to six-member group of stakeholders who will, for an appointed time, hold your corporation or organization's future in their hearts and hands, so to speak. They should be chosen carefully based on the following criteria:

- They are visionary—they can see beyond "what is" to "what if."

- They are complementary—they work well as a team.

- They are discretionary—they are able to keep discussion matters private.

- They are cautionary—they are sensitive to organizational parameters.

In one sense, they are your dream team. They take the raw material handed to them, refine or add additional material, and help you deliver the corporate vision to the community.

## Agree on a Process

What will the end vision look like? That's the job of the builders—the vision team. But just as home builders follow blueprints, the vision team will require some blueprints—a process that will identify the components of the vision and map them into a completed product.

It will surely involve meetings. Person-to-person, eye-to-eye interchange is vital. Whether that is done through video conferencing, in-house committee meetings, or a retreat setting, the give-and-take of the vision team is at the core of the vision-casting process.

## Ways to Notice Hidden Leadership Talent

- Look harder at those who work for you and scrutinize them beyond their weaknesses.

- Look for those who are open and willing to learn new skills and behaviors.

- The best leadership-capable employees aren't afraid to step up to a challenge.

- Those who have hidden leadership capabilities take decisive action and move forward.

- Watch for those who naturally reach out to help others with their work or who seek to collaborate on projects. [2]

## Gather the Facts

A family with five young children traveled along the New England coastline in a crowded minivan. Most of the day's refreshment stops had been at fast-food drive-throughs, so the father was firm in making the decision for the evening meal: "Sit-down, casual dining with seafood—especially crab cakes!"

By the time the family arrived at the restaurant of the father's choice, the majority of the minivan occupants were less than enthusiastic. As they entered the door of the seafood restaurant, a cloud of pessimism and criticism hovered over the group like an approaching thunderstorm.

When the hostess greeted them, the father asked, "Do you serve crabs here?"

The bubbly young lady looked at the disheveled and despondent travelers and replied, "Sure! We serve anyone! Would you like a booth or a table?"

Rule number one for vision casting is to get the *real* picture, not the one that *seems* real. And that will take a gathering of the facts.

- What are the actual numbers?
- Who are the stakeholders?
- Who are the real decision makers?
- Who are the customers?
- What impact are the products and services really making?

You can't make projections on moving forward unless you have a firm grip on where you are and where you've been. A look back at the stats, staffing, programming, and production will give you an analysis of trends that you can use to determine your preferred future.

---

*Rule number one for vision casting is to get the real picture, not the one that seems real.*

---

You will probably need to do a "needs assessment" for developing your ideas. Wikipedia defines a needs assessment as a "systematic process for determining and addressing needs, or 'gaps' between current conditions and desired conditions."

Kansas University's Community Tool Box offers insights on assessing needs: "It's a way of asking group or community members what they see as the most important needs of that group or community. The results of the survey then guide future action."[3]

## Community Tool Box Needs-Assessment Survey Characteristics

- They have a preset list of questions to be answered.

- They have a predetermined sample of the number and types of people to answer these questions chosen in advance.

- They are done by personal interview, phone, or written response (such as a mail-in survey).

- The results of the survey are tabulated, summarized, distributed, discussed, and (last, but not least) used.[4]

## Determine the Readiness for Change

Inevitability, when you cast a vision, not everyone will catch it.

We have a mini lake on our property, and one of the joys of being at home is watching our grandchildren catch fish out of that lake. I don't know who gets more excited (or does more wiggling), the bass or the grandkids, but the end result makes for great memories.

It reminds me of the grandfather and grandson who were fishing. After a long interval of no bites and no fish, the grandson threw his fishing pole on the ground and stomped off. The grandfather caught up to him and asked, "What's the matter?"

The little boy pointed his thumb back toward the lake and said, "The service is lousy!"

Don't be surprised by "lousy service" complaints when it comes to proposed change. Change is a major threat to an established comfort zone. For some people, change means they may...

- have to do something they don't want to do

- have to go somewhere they don't want to go

- lose accrued power they don't want to surrender

- be asked to yield a position they don't want to give up

- lose "real estate" they don't want to liquidate

Sometimes change opens the gate and frees a sacred cow that has been penned in by traditions or opinions.

Mark A. Smith and Larry M. Lindsay address change in their book *Leading Change in Your World*. They identify four stages of change—denial, resistance, exploration, and commitment—and they offer helpful insights for helping people through the process.

- Get them to see that the vision is attainable.
- Transmit the honesty and integrity of the vision.
- Recognize the courage it takes to work through change.
- Cooperate, collaborate, and celebrate every step on the road to change.[5]

## Write the Vision Statement

You've probably heard people say, "I need to see it in writing." Likewise, a vision needs a tangible expression. Once the assessments have been made and the "forward" ideas have been collected, the next step is to write it out in the vision— carefully, correctly, and concisely. It may be capsulized into a small paragraph, but it needs to be a definitive expression of where your organization wants to be, *and it needs to be put into the language of the constituency.*

In other words, it must *motivate and relate*!

## A Results-Focused Story

When your story focuses on results, it will show...

- a culture of optimism
- constancy in purpose
- connection with the team
- creative conflict solutions
- concentration on people
- challenge for learning
- courage to care

## Tell the Story

Everyone likes a good story with a happy ending. Your vision is a happy-ending story. It starts with a compelling history and promises an inspiring future. In between are the steps that will combine the best of the past and the present and turn it into preferred future.

Whether you tell the story in print or in some other media, the presentation must be attractive, interest-grabbing, and *relational*. Your audience wants to know how your vision will affect people, not how it will promote your corporation or organization. Therefore, your story should include information about

satisfied constituents
founders or their family members

statistics that demonstrate growth or change
past and present leaders

## Gain Team Buy-In

What is the first audience you want to impress? Your team, of course! They carry the banner for the organization. They are the frontline soldiers of your mission, so they should be among the first to review the vision. They should know where the organization is going, when it plans to arrive, and how they will be involved in the process.

The vision presentation could even be a team event. Make it a celebration—complete with pizza or donuts and coffee. Once you have convinced those closest to the action that the action plan has value, you are ready to take the message to the rest of your constituency.

## Articulate the Vision

Business leader and author Kevin Cope says, "Customers buy more than just products. They purchase trustworthiness, convenience, prestige, or a memorable experience. Determine what *your* customers are buying."[6]

It is one thing to establish the future; it is another to communicate it in such a way that people want to go there with you. A carefully crafted and articulated vision is a tool for obtaining loyalty from people with a vested interest in the organization. Get them on board first and then communicate your vision as widely as possible.

Chapter 4

# Quality Testing a Vision

*Leaders imagine a future that is better than the
present, and they look for ways to make it happen.*

Two thousand fourteen may be known as the year of the
vehicle recall. General Motors alone recalled more than
30 million vehicles. Here's what we should remember:
Those products were born from a corporate vision. They were
created, developed, manufactured, tested, and released to the
public by the best minds and most diligent laborers in the corporation. But over time, some owners discovered that some
product components had hidden problems that jeopardized
their safety.

Your vision plan may also be subject to recall. Over time,
obsolete or faulty components may surface. Once that happens, it's back to the drawing board. But first, a second look at
the existing vision may indicate some fault lines.

Former president of Coca-Cola Jack Stahl said, "You and
your team must review, understand, and take into account
your organization's strengths, weaknesses, and the environment in which it operates...Develop a clear strategy that

will galvanize people and require them to focus on the right actions for success."[1]

So how does your vision plan measure up? Let's put it through the filter of several criteria.

## Does the Vision Plan Reflect the Values of the Organization?

As I've said, a vision plan must be built on the foundation of your die-for principles—the raw beliefs that propel your organization. Everyone familiar with Chick-fil-A knows it is a values-driven organization. Chick-fil-A's corporate purpose is clearly seen on its website: "To glorify God by being a faithful steward of all that is entrusted to us and to have a positive influence on all who come into contact with Chick-fil-A."[2]

Chuck Salter wrote about the company's value system and especially its customer service.

> Every year Chick-fil-A spends more than $1 million evaluating its service. In addition to traditional focus groups, the company conducts a quarterly phone survey with customers from each restaurant (the incentive: a free sandwich). The 20 or so questions focus on four factors that most affect loyalty according to Chick-fil-A research: taste, speed, attentiveness and courteousness, and cleanliness. Each location receives a two-page report detailing how it's doing in each area and how it

compares to the chain's top performers. In
other words, what's working and what needs
improving. [3]

"Taste, speed, attentiveness and courteousness, and cleanliness" are value standards the company has established to set
it apart from other fast-food companies. What are your organization's standards? An evaluation of your vision plan may
include a checklist of standards that tell you whether you are
being true to your values.

## Does the Vision Plan Motivate People to Leave Their Comfort Zone?

Dr. No wasn't just a character in a James Bond movie—he
might have been the personification of a board member in a
church I pastored early on. "No" was his predictable answer
to items on the church board meeting agenda.

Obviously, Dr. No was firmly planted in his comfort zone.
A fact of leadership life: If you're for it, you can be sure some
people will be against it—unless they can be convinced of the
benefits of moving in its direction.

What are the incentives in your action plan? What components have you embedded in the plan to draw people (particularly the stakeholders) out of their comfort zone? They
may include...

added value,
increased revenue,

increased influence, or
proven acceptance.

Remember, it's a people-driven vision plan, so you must test your vision's ability to meet people's felt or real needs.

A sign posted in an eighteenth-century church held a message that will always be relevant:

> *A vision without a task is but a dream.*
> *A task without a vision is drudgery.*
> *A vision and a task is the hope of the world.*

## Does the Vision Plan Generate Feelings of Hope?

The third test of vision-plan effectiveness is in its unwrapping. When a vision is unwrapped, it should bring a sense of hope. Anyone who has watched children unwrap Christmas presents knows when the gift is on-target. It can be seen on the faces and heard in the expressions of those who are unwrapping. There is a *Wow!* factor that can't be explained, just enjoyed.

Watch the same children open a package of clothing and a package containing a toy. Compare their reaction—the toy almost always wins.

> *From changing times to changing technology, our world is ever evolving. So a periodic update of strategic plans is important.*

Friend and church consultant Dan Reiland says, "Mission will give people purpose. Values will give people character. Vision will give people direction." The Christmas package of clothing is practical and ultimately valuable, but it doesn't provide a child the same hopeful future as a PlayStation or Xbox.

Why not use the test of expression? Discover how people react when you first unwrap your vision and then again after a while. The *Wow!* factor may reveal whether your vision plan is on-target.

## Does the Vision Plan Create Openness to Change?

Sheryl Sandberg, COO of Facebook and former Google executive, wrote a controversial but highly regarded book called *Lean In: Women, Work, and the Will to Lead*. *Forbes* magazine contributor Kerry Hannon pointed out five of Sandberg's best tips.

- Be more open to taking career risks. Shift from thinking "I'm not ready to do that" to "I want to do that."

- Skip the people pleasing. Push back on things, challenging others' decisions.

- Visualize your career as a jungle gym, not a ladder. Ladders are limiting. Jungle gyms offer more creative exploration.

- Allow yourself to fantasize about your career. Have a long-term dream. Ask yourself, "What can I do to improve myself at work?"

- Start a Lean In circle. Form a peer group of eight to ten people who offer encouragement and development ideas.[4]

Argenti and Forman say a vision "must be re-envisioned, flexible, and responsive to changing opportunities."[5]

Put windows in your vision plan. That is, word it (or reword it) in a way that lets in fresh sunlight. From changing times to changing technology, our world is ever evolving. So a periodic update of strategic plans is important.

Openness to change is contagious. Once the leader and the team exhibit it, the rest of the stakeholders will be more apt to buy in.

### Does the Vision Plan Clarify the Cause?

In a book on management lessons learned from the Apple Corporation, Jeffrey L. Cruikshank summarized some highs and lows in Apple's planning process. One bulleted summary advised, "Beware of creeping elegance...Don't let your products start to exaggerate themselves."[6]

The lesson can be applied to an organization's vision plan

as well. If the leadership isn't careful, the plan can develop legs. It can go beyond the established parameters of funding, staffing, facilities, and so forth.

Jay Stein, chairman and CEO of Stein Mart, offered this advice:

> Grow slowly. We got to 10 stores and said, "Perhaps we can open 10 more." Don't wake up one morning and say you want 100 stores, because you'll stretch yourself and your resources too quickly.[7]

When that happens, the core cause is often lost. Values are traded for *valuables*. Check to make sure the vision or its revision has not been muddied. Invite your vision team or other stakeholders to check it for accuracy.

A *Detroit Free Press* article gave a clue as to why identifying the cause is important to vision casting—especially when a specific audience is identified. It cites the rising influence of the millennial generation, the 18–34 age group.

> Stores are selling more cause-related products because millennials have a commitment to giving back to society in some way—37% of millennials are likely to purchase an item associated with a cause, compared with 30% of non-millennials, according to a 2012 study by the Boston Consulting Group…At least 70%

of millennials have purchased a product that supports a cause. And they're more willing to pay extra for a product if it supports a cause they also support.[8]

## Does the Vision Plan Resource a Common Direction?

Everyone who has been in a wedding or has attended a wedding likely has a story to tell. The groom faints, and the groomsmen fall like dominoes. The bride slips and falls on the dance floor. The wedding party is posing on the dock when it falls into the lake. These scenarios make the nuptials memorable. One of my favorites is of the couple who wanted to include a unity candle in the wedding ceremony.

Three candles are placed on a stand. The bride and groom take the two outer candles, which are lit, and combine them to light the unlit center candle, symbolizing the unity of their faith. Then they blow out their individual candles as a sign of surrendering their individual freedom.

But on this occasion, the groom had some second thoughts when it came to blowing out his candle. He whispered loudly to the minister, "Is it okay if we just blow out *her* candle?"

Is everyone still on board your Vision Express? Or are some people hesitant to blow out their freedom candle? Another vision quality test is to see if the stakeholders are still going in its proposed direction.

Following its launch, the impact of your vision plan should be evaluated, not only to see if the organization is on course but also to determine whether the organization has popularized and utilized the direction successfully.

- Is there an ongoing familiarity with its content?

- Are its principles displayed in the actions of stakeholders?

- Are any watered-down versions circulating?

- Is there a continued optimism about its effectiveness?

## Does the Vision Plan Outlive Its Visionary?

Author and college president David L. McKenna says, "At each stage of institutional change, the leader must stop and ask the question about matching personal gifts with the management style needed for the next stage of organizational development."[9]

The last quality test of a vision is how it will survive its visionary. Every organization should have a survival plan in place, not only for surviving a calamity but also for surviving a vacancy. Medicine is doing its best to keep leaders fit forever, but even the fittest aren't immune to a debilitating illness. What is the shelf life of the vision plan once the visionary is on the shelf? McKenna says, "Interviews with great leaders confirm that these leaders speak their long-term vision in general terms but have a precise understanding of what must be done today."[10]

Do you have a "vision insurance policy"? Not so much to guard against loss, but to assure the long-range viability of your vision plan.

- What general terms will be preserved?
- What corporate values will be guarded?
- What standards and practices will be passed along?

It's never too late to start planning the organizational transition. Just be sure the vision plan is as ready as the team.

What skills do you need to cast a vision and to guide your corporation or organization along the path to success? I'll describe them in the next chapter.

Chapter 5

# Vision Skills

*A-level leaders are not threatened by*
*great potential. They look for it, seek*
*it, recruit it, and develop it.*

A six-foot-eight college student applied for a summer position as a lifeguard. During the interview he was asked about his qualifications.

"Do you have CPR training?"

"Nope," he answered.

"Do you have a first-aid certificate?"

"Nope."

"Do you have any lifeguard experience at all?" The atmosphere grew tense when the applicant gave the same reply. The interviewer said, "Son, I'm almost afraid to ask, but can you even swim?"

The lanky student's face brightened. "No, but I can wade pretty far out in the water!"

Leading the vision charge for any organization calls for a skill set that includes more than "wading pretty far out." The leader must be qualified in at least five areas:

    leadership skills
    communication skills
    change skills
    alignment skills
    team skills

Your task as a leader is straightforward:

- Envision organizational objectives and attainable goals.

- Create a vision plan to reach the objectives and goals.

- Recruit, train, and lead a motivated team to implement the vision plan.

- Cast a team vision and obtain team and stakeholder buy-in through effective communications.

- Supervise team tasks, evaluate results, and reward team achievements.

---

*Leaders are visionary followers.*

---

Let's zoom in to discover the skill set a leader needs to bring vision to reality.

## Leadership Skills

There may be as many definitions of leadership as there are politicians at a Fourth of July picnic. Allow me to throw my hat in the ring.

> Leaders are visionary followers who utilize learned and natural skills in influencing others to be the best they can be, to do the best they can do, and to reach a predetermined goal for the betterment of others.

**Leaders are visionary followers.** The art of leading is always preceded by the art of following. By watching the dreamers, they learn to dream. By serving the leaders, they learn to lead. Following is a learned skill that is born from a mix of humility, loyalty, and service.

John C. Maxwell is more than a friend to me—he is a mentor. In serving as his first staff person, I learned to live large and think big. I watched as his dream turned to a reality beyond what either of us saw at first. As the first vice president of his Injoy organization, I was privileged to observe the building of an international leadership training network from the ground up. Following John inspired me to be a leader.

## 19 Characteristics of Leaders

1. They accept others.
2. They are flexible.
3. They enjoy challenges.
4. They are self-aware.
5. They value giftedness in others.
6. They are courageous.
7. They are supportive of others.

8. They keep agreements.

9. They share information freely.

10. They listen.

11. They facilitate others.

12. They understand group dynamics.

13. They understand process improvement.

14. They know how to manage meetings.

15. They know how to manage projects.

16. They give feedback.

17. They let go of personal agendas.

18. They resolve conflicts.

19. They are good communicators.

To adapt a golf expression, leaders "go to school" on the experiences of others. Just as an amateur golfer watches a pro golfer's ball placement, swing, follow-through, or putt, you can watch the life and leadership experiences of other leaders.

- How do they teach others?

- What is their attitude toward success or failure?

- What people skills mark their leadership?

- What habits influence their leadership development?

- What techniques do they use to motivate others?

Their ups and downs are lessons in patience, productivity, and perseverance—curriculum modules for future leaders.

**Leaders utilize learned and natural skills.** The debate over natural or developed leadership traits goes on. Personally, I think it is a combination of both, plus the circumstances where people are forced into leadership.

For example, a baseball player may be born with agility, but agility alone is not a substitute for technique. Agility will get the player to the fly ball in a hurry, and technique will enable a good catch. And some agility comes from being forced to jump above an outfield fence to steal a home run!

The fact is, if a leader is to excel in casting a vision and motivating stakeholders, he or she will need to utilize both natural and learned skills.

> Champions work on their skills. They take what's been given to them and perfect it. They may not win the Golden Glove awards. They may not even wear a championship ring. But they are winners because they are improvers.[1]

Remember the library bus? To avid readers in small communities without access to a large library, the traveling library was almost as welcome as an ice-cream truck. Some libraries might still have one, but technology has made the largest libraries in the world available with just a click. A learning leader has a list of books to read, podcasts to listen to, or videos to watch (such as TED talks).

> *One may be a leader for a time, but by helping others succeed, that one will be a leader forever.*
>
> **CHINESE PROVERB**

**Leaders influence people to be their best and do their best.** A good vision plan handed off to a weak team isn't exactly a recipe for success. Leaders are strength coaches. Team strengthening depends on discovering and developing team skills.

Leadership and teaching are twin duties. A gardener doesn't raise roses by the crop. He raises the flowers one bloom at a time. Leadership isn't just about charts and meetings and business plans; it's about influencing lives one person at a time.

People are affected not only by your skills but also by the way you live. The greatest lessons you will ever teach will come from your own experience. Your transparency will be a greater source of inspiration than your facts or theories.

**Leaders are concerned with reaching a predetermined goal for the betterment of others.** The end result of every vision plan objective or subsequent activity is the positive difference it makes in the lives of people. George Hathaway said, "In the end, leadership is all about people. It's about how we treat one another, how we communicate effectively, how we respect each other, and how we earn the trust of those we lead. After all, leadership is really about only one thing—helping others to succeed at what they do."[2]

## Communication Skills

If you are in leadership, you are in communications. It doesn't just come with the territory—it *is* the territory. Every area of your leadership will demand good global, corporate, or personal communication. You can build the world's greatest widget, but unless you communicate its unique existence, your widget will soon smell like mothballs—the odor of being put on the shelf. You can write the most complete and courageous vision plan ever conceived, but unless you communicate it, it is a passing fancy—and there isn't much of a market for antique fancies.

Michael Hyatt, noted author, publisher, and blogger, said it right: "We don't need more messages or products or services. Instead, we need *better* messages, products, and services. Specifically, we need those that wow."[3]

Your communication tasks include *thinking, writing, delivering*, and *repeating* the values and objectives of the organization. Your communication toolbox may include...

> texts and e-mails
> social media
> websites

  blogs and columns
  flyers and brochures
  news releases
  letters and notes
  exhibits
  podcasts
  live presentations

Each has its own goal, target audience, and expected impact. And each demands your research, study, and improved technique.

There are more how-to resources for print and online communications than I could ever cover—or you could ever absorb. Rather than focusing on the fine strokes of methodology, let me give you a few broad strokes on effective communication.

**Effective communication begins with a perceived *who*.** Your audience isn't the ambiguous airwaves or the printed page. Your audience is people—people of all levels of education and influence, people of all cultures, beliefs, age groups, and attention spans. Who are they? You need to know them in order to gain their attention. Other factors, such as their technical savvy, will determine your message and your delivery method.

**Effective communication is built on the *what* and *why*.** *What* do you need to communicate—a product, service, program, initiative, building, or staffing change? Whatever it is, your communication needs to be inspiring enough to draw attention, detailed enough to provoke thought, and personal enough to motivate loyalty. *Why* are you releasing the communication? Is it to gain buy-in? Are you seeking financial support? Do you need customer feedback? The *what* and *why* questions are essential steps to consider before production.

**Effective communication is filtered through a *when* and *how*.** Timing is everything whether you are a stand-up comic or a corporate communicator. Communication released too soon could be a vision killer. Communication released too late could be a time waster.

How will you release your information? What media best fits your audience? And speaking of *how*, what staffing (paid or volunteer) will you need? Will you outsource the production work or carry that load in-house?

---

### Seven Keys to Becoming a Great Communicator

- Research your topic.
- Examine your motive.
- Know your environment.
- Plan your use of media.

- Develop your own unique style.
- Engage your audience.
- Know your objectives.[4]

**Effective communication speaks at the common level.** Another important tool in your communications toolbox is humor. Author Bob Whipple visualizes humor as a friendly dog's wagging tail and calls it the "wag factor." He says leaders should have a good ratio of wag over bark in their communications.

Granville N. Toogood, in his book *The Articulate Executive*, uses this story to illustrate how effective humor can be in communicating or in controlling a situation. Former Secretary of State Alexander Haig was speaking at the United Nations when some South American nationalists began to heckle him from the first row of the balcony.

> Without missing a beat, Haig stopped his speech just long enough to say that he was unable to hear what the men in the balcony were trying to say, but "if you would just step forward a few feet I'm sure I could hear you a lot better." The audience laughed, and the hecklers sat down and stopped heckling.[5]

Toogood says there are three rules for using humor:

- Tell the story as if it were true.
- Tell the story to make a point.
- Tell the story correctly.

Let me add several other principles.

*Use humor carefully.* A well-rehearsed, well-considered joke or story must be a bridge that links to a principle. The common expression applies here: What's your point? Ask yourself some important questions:

- To whom am I speaking?
- What is the most positive way to say it?
- What is the most interesting way to say it?

*Use humor sensitively.* Attack-dog humor will do more harm than help. If you need a foil, let it be you. Your communication task is to build up rather than tear down. Mean-spirited, stereotypical stories are always out of place. Also, family members are off-limits. If you use personal stories, get permission first!

*Use humor skillfully.* A forgotten punch line, a failure to include pertinent story details, or a failure to speak distinctly can result in a pregnant pause that gives birth to an embarrassing moment of silence.

## Effective Humor

- It must be relevant—the audience must understand the topic.

- It must have an obvious punch line.

- It must be well timed.

- It must be concise.

- It must have a payoff.

*Use humor occasionally.* A steady line of stories, one-liners, or jokes is no substitute for careful preparation. The speaker who tries to compete with the Comedy Channel will find himself or herself subject to the mental remote button of the audience.

*Use humor effectively.* Learn from the comedy pros. What is conspicuous about their delivery? Timing? Eye contact? Material? Reaction to "bombs"? But learn without obviously copying their mannerisms. Humor should be an extension of your own personality.

*Use humor selectively.* Humor must fit the demographics of the audience. A story about DVDs, for instance, will flop if its told to high schoolers, who are more familiar with streaming video or audio downloads. The speaker should always try to communicate at the audience's level of understanding.

## Change Skills

Leaders are landscapers—they have to move mountains and molehills of opinion, tradition, and succession to give their vision plan curb appeal. If the leader proposes change that doesn't meet the felt needs of the target audience, it won't attract loyalty. And your own attitude toward change will affect the change climate enormously.

Businessman and management professor Harry M. Jansen Kraemer Jr. highlights four phases or attitudes of leadership and change.

- *Reactive.* The reactive leader "spends the majority of his time trying to duplicate what everybody else is doing."

- *Tolerant.* "A leader who only tolerates change does what she can to avoid it, but will adapt when she has no other alternative."

- *Accepting.* "A leader who accepts change looks at the situation more positively and realizes that the organization will be better off."

- *Proactive.* "Instead of only reacting to, tolerating, or accepting change grudgingly, the proactive leader is actually initiating it…A proactive attitude toward change enables leaders to be the most effective."[6]

There are at least five types of change:

- *Tentative*—change that requires only minimal fine-tuning.

- *Turbulent*—change that is extreme and may cause emotional or organizational chaos.

- *Tactical*—change that enhances existing systems.

- *Transitional*—change that includes immediate and necessary organizational movement.

- *Transformative*—change that people catch, cooperate with, and propagate.

All change requires five leadership skills. The leader must be able to...

1. evaluate change in relation to the organization's values and mission

2. communicate the *what*, *why*, *when*, and *how* of a change

3. produce a concise and continual flow of information (Informed people are happy people.)

4. personalize and present a sensitive and logical "elevator pitch" to stakeholders

5. create and maintain an environment of respect, openness, and acceptance of other opinions

Gina Hernez-Broome and Richard L. Hughes wrote, "Twenty years ago leadership was determined by two factors—task and relationship behaviors. Today's leadership can be described as transformational."[7]

## Alignment Skills

I read that planes fly off course 90 percent of the time. As someone with almost as many frequent flyer miles as a seagull, that statistic didn't exactly warm my heart, but it's probably true. The pilot's ultimate goal is to land the plane at the right airport at the right time. To do that, he or she needs to be able to map the route, factor in the weather, and utilize technology that keeps the plane on course.

It's about alignment.

Leaders who move people toward a preferred organizational future must have vertical and horizontal alignment skills.

*Vertical skill* relates to attitude and belief. Leaders must know where they are coming from in order to take people to the place (they believe) they should go. They must first understand themselves.

Do they have confidence in their intellectual, emotional, and physical skill and in their position?

Do they have an inner confidence in their spiritual skill, their faith in and dependence on God? In other words, what is their leadership fuel?

*Horizontal skill* relates to the leader's relationships with people. For a leader to survive, he or she must examine and address four important questions:

1. Will this strategy help us hit the target?

2. Do people support this strategy, and do they understand the target?

3. Will this strategy utilize the people and their gifts in reaching the target?

4. Is this strategy in line with the mission?

True leaders are "people" leaders. They understand who people are, what they want, how to motivate them to be involved, and how to move them in a cooperative and values-driven direction.

## Team Skills

New employees at Nordstrom stores are handed a binder with a message on the cover that includes this:

> We crave support from our colleagues. We know that the health of our relationships is paramount to our own success, and that the joy of sharing ideas leads to a diversity of options. Our reward is access to a wealth of knowledge that we would have otherwise overlooked.[8]

A vision is of little value if left in a folder or on a hard drive. It is of greater value when it is put into the hands of people with capable minds and bodies, people who are willing to do the finish work. And the finish work is under the supervision of the leader/contractor.

As a leader you will need six essential skills for developing a vision plan team:

1. *Delegation.* Delegation involves setting expectations, providing direction, allowing for creativity, negotiating deadlines, checking on results, and rewarding performance.

2. *Affirmation.* Every team needs people with a variety of skills. If you honor only the shot makers but never the shot takers, your team will lose momentum. Whom you applaud, you empower. Cheer for your team.

3. *Provision.* When a person is given the resources to succeed, he or she will feel a part of the team. When you delegate, ask, "Do you have everything you need?" You'll gain a long-term contributor.

4. *Motivation.* People are motivated by many things, including money, guilt, and recognition. But the best motivation is fueled by convincing team members that their efforts have added value—that people's lives will be forever changed by their actions.

5. *Evaluation.* If you're interested in team success, you'll need to evaluate its performance. Did we

reach our goal? What could have been done better? How will we avoid making the same mistake next time? What can I do to improve results? Ask these questions regularly.

6. *Celebration.* When your team has a victory, celebrate! Point out the contribution of each member. Never let a milestone go by unnoticed. Find a reason to cheer. Celebrating wins will energize your team.

I read of a Denver, Colorado, high school football team whose record was 1–0 before the team took the field for their first game. Their coach explained that each year during their training camp, he assigns the team a community work project. He explained that the team bonds around the philosophy, "You don't give to get, you get to give." The community project helps them work together as a team as they better society, and as a result they are one of Colorado's winningest teams. That's the personification of leadership skill in vision planning—inspiring a team to work together to make a meaningful contribution to other people.

Good coaching technique is important to people development. Let's talk about good coaching techniques next.

Part 2

# Leadership That Relates

## Chapter 6

# Coaching Objectives

*Great leaders are not leaders of*
*followers. They are leaders of leaders.*

Y ou can make an impact in two ways. One is to run into
someone. The other is to lead them—and carry them
if necessary. Hunter Gandee chose to lead and to carry.

Wanting to raise awareness about cerebral palsy, fourteen-
year-old Hunter walked 40 miles with Braden—his seven-
year-old brother and a cerebral palsy victim—strapped to his
back. Hunter determined to put a face on the muscular disor-
der by carrying Braden from Temperance, Ohio, to the University of Michigan campus in Ann Arbor.

The walk was strenuous, and Hunter fought fatigue,
extreme heat, and then rain to carry his 50-pound brother.
He said he thought about quitting after 30 miles, but a phone
call from a friend convinced him to go on. During the call, the
friend prayed with him, strengthening him in spirit. After-
ward, Hunter and Braden rested, changed Braden's position
to prevent additional chaffing, and then continued the walk.

Family members and friends waited at the destination

point at the top of a hill on the campus. The finish line was a large banner that read, "Go Blue!" When Hunter and Braden reached the top, Hunter lifted his young brother so he could touch the banner. Hunter was interviewed about the trek and said, "We pushed through it. And we're here!"[1]

The next summer, Hunter and Braden topped their effort by trekking 57 miles. Fifteen supporters walked with them the entire way.[2]

The story is a vivid illustration of how leaders...

- envision the finish line

- carry others on their shoulders

- fight through adversity to reach a destination or goal

- are strengthened by the encouragement of others, even as they encourage

- make midcourse adjustments

- share their win with others

Leaders lead by *principle* and coach by *application*. They develop the team as they journey with them to the organizational destination. If you are in a place of leadership, you are a coach. That is both a substantial responsibility and an awesome opportunity!

The coaching paradigm is twenty-first-century leadership at its best. Its objectives are to...

train players
build winning relationships
give and receive feedback
monitor performance
motivate to win

Former Coca-Cola president Jack Stahl offers this overview of coaching.

> I cannot emphasize enough how necessary
> it is for you to coach the people you believe
> have strong potential for your organization,
> encouraging them early in their careers to seek
> a variety of jobs and projects, where they have
> the opportunity and enough time in each role
> to learn the core skills that will be critical to
> achieving success throughout their careers.[3]

Four words describe the scope of coaching: leading, mentoring, relating, and training. Let's unpack that.

## Leading

People do what people see. The phrase, "Leadership is caught, not taught" is as much of a classic as a '57 Chevy, but I would suggest that both teaching and catching are important in leadership development. Leadership characteristics are usually mirrored in the lives of those whom a leader leads.

*The coaching paradigm is twenty-
first-century leadership at its best.*

One of my leadership heroes is Melvin M. Maxwell, a former college professor and president, an author, and the father of John C. Maxwell. I've told the story on many occasions that when John and I were in college, his father took us to Positive Mental Attitude rallies in nearby Dayton, Ohio, to hear well-known motivational speakers, including Norman Vincent Peale, Earl Nightingale, W. Clement Stone, and Zig Ziglar. They impacted my life with their teaching, but Dr. Maxwell impacted my life with his *living* as well. I first learned to lead others by watching him lead—in classrooms, in boardrooms, and in the car on the way to hear one of those great speakers.

## Characteristics of the Successful Leader-Coaches

- They are good managers of their time and resources.
- They have a sense of mission.
- They are able to help teams focus.
- They see their coworkers as teammates.
- They work from a game plan.

- They position team members according to their strengths.
- They define team expectations.

## Mentoring

Mentoring is the process of adding value to people's lives. Almost every facet of coaching could be defined as mentoring: *inspiration*, *instruction*, *correction*, and *delegation*. But every mentee comes to the table carrying unique baggage. The coach's job is to open it with their permission and find out what can be used or repurposed to motivate them to effectiveness and excellence. Former IBM manager George Hathaway described the leader's relationship with his or her team:

> Every good leader understands the fact that his or her employees are, first of all, human. They have feelings. They want to be treated with respect. They have opinions that must be heard. They know that they are not perfect, but they are good people who deserve to be treated as such.[4]

**Mentors inspire.** A *Fortune* magazine cover featured this quote from former president Bill Clinton: "More people can be great leaders than think they can, but they need a purpose greater than themselves."

A mentor affirms mentees' strengths, sometimes in the face of their denial. My friend Ron McClung blogged the story of Willie Mays, who began his professional baseball career with only one hit in his first 26 at bats. He said Mays's manager once found him in the dugout, crying after a poor batting performance. Asking Mays what was the matter, the baseball legend said he belonged in the minors, not the big leagues. McClung said his manager, Leo Durocher, put his arm around the discouraged player and replied, "As long as I'm manager of the Giants, you'll be my center fielder."[5]

Mays went on to hit 660 home runs in the stellar career that followed. He simply needed a mentor who believed in him and was willing to let him know it. As others have said, treat people as if they were what they ought to be, and you may help them to become what they are capable of being.

**Mentors instruct.** Mentors are teachers. They relate and motivate by sharing knowledge. Willie Mays didn't become a home-run king by the compliment alone. You can be sure that even as his coach affirmed his place in the majors, he had a training regimen in mind. Telling someone *what* to do, without knowing whether they know *how* to do it, isn't real leadership.

> *Few things help an individual more than to place responsibility upon him, and to let him know you trust him.*
>
> **BOOKER T. WASHINGTON**

**Mentors correct.** The twenty-first century has seen epic upheavals in the world of sports. Professional athletes' large salaries, star status, and other benefits have roused the beasts of inner greed and anger. Such organizations as the NFL, NBA, and MLB have had to deal firmly with players who have crossed the boundaries of acceptable behavior.

The frontline soldiers in dealing with errant athletes are their coaches. Behind the locker-room doors and in their private offices, coaches use their parenting and leadership skills. The results are often announced in minimalistic sentences, such as "We had a discussion about that," or "I think we're clear about that." Both suggest that the coach got his or her point across to the player.

Mentors know that unacceptable behavior cannot be accepted. They kindly but firmly and privately...

> gather the facts
> explore the motives
> address the specific issue
> reinforce organizational values
> explain the alternatives
> expect corrected behavior
> affirm corrected behavior

**Mentors delegate.** Mentoring allows mentees to learn by doing. In his book *Simply Rich*, Amway cofounder Rich DeVos explains that his family has a private holding company, apart from Amway, that was created to pass along business principles and ethics to its next generation of leaders. At age 16, DeVos family members are inducted into the private company, and at 25, they become voting members. Its constitutional activities include required training in leadership and family values.

DeVos said, "We are very intentional about trying to come together, meet together, spend time together multigenerationally, and involve and engage future generations at appropriate times in the affairs of the family, as well as the activities of the business."[6]

## Relating

Have you ever noticed that a puppy can relate to just about anyone? Puppies may be awkward and a bit sloppy. They may be impulsive and may not know how to react to some situations. But give a crowd of even the most sophisticated people a puppy, and their inner child will emerge faster than the puppy's bark.

I've always thought that puppies could teach leaders and coaches a thing or two about relating to people.

*Puppies are glad to see you.* They're not concerned about where you've been or what you've done; they just care that you are with them. Coaching is about celebrating people as they are and where they are. When your mentee knows that you are more concerned with their *presence* than their past, you have already begun to relate and motivate.

*Puppies don't have hidden agendas.* Puppies give without

expecting anything in return. The wag of the tail, the sloppy kiss, the jumping up to greet you…none of that costs you. If you want to truly relate to others as a leader-coach, get rid of any hidden agendas.

I like the story of the young lady who broke up with her boyfriend but later had a change of heart.

> Dear Fred, I've been so upset since our breakup that I haven't been able to eat or sleep or watch TV or even spend time on Facebook. The more I think about our relationship, the more I realize how important you are to me. Can you ever find it in your heart to forgive me?
>
> Alice
>
> P.S. BTW, congratulations on winning the lottery! See ya soon!

*Puppies aren't concerned with your accomplishments.* Puppies don't love you because of your degrees or honors—they love you for who you are. Coaching that relates doesn't choose favorites. It is culturally blind and decidedly inclusive. George Hathaway said, "Do your very best not to act in a way that signals your preference for one employee over another. Small steps like remembering to alphabetize all distribution lists will keep everyone guessing."[7]

*Puppies are loyal.* Puppies will love you whether you feed them gourmet dog food in a designer dish or table scraps on a paper plate. They don't practice conditional loyalty—and neither should the leader-coach. If you want to relate to people, they must know that you are unconditionally loyal—that you'll be the first in and the last out in times of adversity.

*Puppies are enthusiastic.* A puppy does everything with unabated enthusiasm. And that's one thing that draws people to them. Of course, they can be overzealous at times, but we're all glad they err in that direction. Enthusiasm is a *great* motivator! Teach enthusiasm by your example and watch how quickly people catch it.

## Training

*Forbes* magazine researched corporate spending on training in 2013. "US spending on corporate training grew by 15% last year (the highest growth rate in seven years) to over $70 billion in the US and over $130 billion worldwide." Why the increase?

> Organizations today suffer from a "skills supply chain" challenge. Not only do more than 70% of organizations cite "capability gaps" as one of their top five challenges, but many companies also tell us that it takes 3-5 years to take a seasoned professional and make them fully productive. [8]

No matter the size of your organization—or your budget—you simply can't afford to postpone training. Coaches have an opportunity to relate to and motivate others through an intentional training regimen. From my experience, I believe that regimen must incorporate at least four key areas:

- values and ethics
- attitude and interpersonal relationships
- planning and communications
- technique and service

**Values and ethics.** One of the most important things a coach can convey is that all workers and leaders stand on the shoulders of others. They are products of the environment in which they were trained. They are here because they own the organization's basic beliefs and best practices. Bestselling author and teacher Dave Ramsey outlined seven life lessons he learned from the late Chick-fil-A founder, Truett Cathy.

1. Define your values and stick to them.
2. A little customer service goes a long way.
3. Make family a priority.
4. Know why you exist.
5. Plan ahead.
6. Invest in others.
7. Don't be afraid to start small.[9]

Cathy focused on things that never change. Ramsey cites the founder's commitment to close his restaurants on Sunday to rest and to honor the Lord's Day. You can be sure that every company trainee is introduced to the policy and its values from the very beginning.

Ethical practices come from the organization's value system. Those predetermined boundaries give leaders and managers security, but they also give them an obligation to pass the information on through the ranks.

**Attitude and interpersonal relationships.** Joining a team doesn't necessarily make you a team member. Someone can join a team legally and physically without joining it emotionally. A coach's responsibility is to develop team loyalty—helping people make the emotional connection with their associates. The late comedian Rodney Dangerfield had a slogan that became his brand—"I get no respect." One objective of coaching is to teach team members that respect is integral to interpersonal relationships.

The first area of respect is *self-respect*. At the core of good attitude and good interpersonal relationships is a healthy opinion of self. A personal-skills evaluation, led by a caring coach, can go a long way in helping team members discover what they *can* do. Someone whose thinking is being healed can learn to respect others.

In my book *ReThink Your Life*, I talk about the importance of filling your mind with the right fuel. "In order to have healthy minds, we must have healthy thoughts. Just as the health of our bodies depends, in part, on the content of the foods we consume, the fitness of our minds correlates with the healthiness of the ideas we embrace."[10]

**Planning and communications.** In a takeoff of the classic "teach someone to fish" advice, I'd suggest, "Teach someone to *plan*, and you feed them for a lifetime." The long-term welfare of any future leader is determined by their ability to build, launch, and communicate a carefully thought-out vision plan. So an additional coaching objective is to teach team members how to develop short- and long-range plans that will set a *destination* and *direction*. Additionally, they must understand the importance of setting objectives and goals for the journey.

The famous Yogi Berra line "If you don't know where you're going...you might not get there" is gold-standard advice. Along with that, if you don't *tell* people where you're going, you might not get them to follow you there.

Team members must be taught that they are *messengers of the mission*—that the public audience or stakeholder buy-in of a mission depends on the team telling the story. In other words, if they don't sell it, nobody's buying it.

Modern coaching is teaching the team to use modern technology and old-fashioned salesmanship to sell the vision.

**Technique and service.** Placing an order at many local fast-food restaurants provides a vivid example of the need for teaching people how to treat customers. Granted, with high employee turnover, managers are challenged to squeeze in a minimum training experience *before* the employees turn in their name tags! But poor customer service characterizes many establishments. Yet some companies excel. In a book I coauthored with Keith Hawk, *Terrific! Five Star Customer Service*, we offer this caution:

> Instead of asking, "How can I serve you?" then after the response saying, "We can make that happen," some ask, "What do you want?" and say (or infer), "No, let me tell you what you want." At the end of the day, the customer will go across the street to someone who will provide what he or she actually wants.[11]

People who *serve* find the need and make the commitment to fill it. People with *technique* use intellectual property and mechanical ability to implement the commitment.

---

### Characteristics of Terrific! Customer Service

- Find out what the customer really wants.

- Honor the customer.

- Confirm the customer.

- Do a little bit more.[12]

You don't have to manufacture and market widgets to serve customers. Anything you offer (including ideas, projects, or services) calls for people to buy in. The coach has an objective to teach team members to always believe the customer is always right.

Yes—the leadership journey has a few bumps in the road now and then. I'll tell you how to overcome some prevailing challenges in the next chapter.

Chapter 7

# Overcoming Leadership Challenges

*Leadership is about gaining enough
knowledge and wisdom to move people
and plans from obscurity to excellence.*

The story is told of a man who bought his first boat. It was shiny, new, powerful, and expensive. He couldn't wait to launch it and show it off to his friends. But no matter what he did, the boat just wouldn't respond. It was sluggish. It wouldn't plane. He just couldn't maneuver it. He looked around the boat and checked everything topside, but everything seemed to be working.

Seeing his plight, the mechanic from the marina where he bought the boat motored out to him. Soon the mechanic was in the water, checking underneath the boat, trying to find the problem. Immediately he surfaced and said to the new boat owner, "I think I've spotted the problem. We recommend you take the boat *off* the trailer before you head out into the lake!"

Publisher and author Michael Hyatt posted the "Top-10

Characteristics of Lousy Leaders" on his highly acclaimed *Intentional Leadership* blog:

1. They don't have enough confidence to lead at their level.

2. They're arrogant, assuming they always know what's best.

3. They're disorganized.

4. Their words and actions erode trust, even with their supporters.

5. They over-promise and under-deliver.

6. They don't articulate a clear vision.

7. They don't enroll others in their initiatives.

8. They're not transparent.

9. They're blind to what's happening in their own organizations.

10. They don't hold people accountable—especially themselves.[1]

I like the story of the executive who had a travel day full of delays and cancelled flights on his way to a corporate meeting in Philadelphia. His schedule was wrecked, and his luggage missed the last flight and was on its way to Detroit. It was past midnight when he finally landed and caught the shuttle for a 30-minute drive to the hotel. He checked in and wearily made his way to the elevator. Reaching the tenth floor of the hotel, he began searching for his room key. He was still searching when the elevator door closed. He searched his pockets and then his briefcase but still couldn't find it.

Exhausted, he pushed the elevator button again and made his way to the front desk. "Ma'am," he said to the receptionist. "Could you tell me which room I'm in?"

She replied with a smile and then a look of concern, "Why yes, sir. This is the lobby."

---

*Leadership isn't just about reaching a destination; it's also about overcoming some frustrating obstacles along the way.*

---

Every leader will experience variations of that kind of a day. Leadership isn't just about reaching a destination; it's also about overcoming some frustrating obstacles along the way. How you face your obstacles will determine the impact and duration of your leadership.

I think there are at least four main areas of leadership challenges.

## Unfinished Work

Practically your whole life has been affected by the theme of finishing what you start. If you're like me, it started in childhood at the breakfast table—"Finish your cereal." Maybe the snap and crackle were already reduced to a hum, but you finished it off and made your way to school.

The teacher greeted you with a smile (or not). You settled at your desk, and before long your teacher asked, "Class, how many of you have completed your reading assignment?" Guilty as charged!

You carried the guilt home with you and changed clothes for some serious playtime. But before you can make your escape, Mother asks, "Did you finish your homework?" And on and on, through college and into your career, you are faced with the same line of questioning.

There are at least three principles that apply to unfinished work:

*1. You can do some things better than everything.* If you push back from the desk, you might see that some of your work isn't an immediate necessity. It may look urgent. But unless it threatens the welfare of your employment or national security, it might fit better on tomorrow's schedule than today's.

*2. Some of your work is rooted in perceived importance rather than real.* In other words, your "work journey" might actually be a guilt trip. Your plate may have some table scraps from someone else's plate on it. You're doing work for a friend in need. You're doing work to impress another (or yourself). You're doing work for a perceived reward.

*3. Unfinished work doesn't equal failed work.* If it's unfinished, it's simply in the finishing stages. Tomorrow you'll have a second chance to do what you intended to do today. Reexamine its priority in light of your vision. Change your setting. Think about the possibilities and begin again.

## Unmet Expectations

Many folks spend most of their lives trying to meet secondhand standards. Someone sets a bar (that they inherited from another) and then expects everyone under or around them to reach that bar. W. Clement Stone wrote, "There is little difference in people, but that little difference makes a big difference. The little difference is attitude. The big difference is whether it is positive or negative."

You were diligent in framing your vision, identifying your objective, setting your goals, and launching your vision plan. Then out of nowhere you take a left hook to the chin when a team member fails or a promised funding doesn't materialize. You imagine the critics holding up their scorecards, the naysayers whispering "I told you so," and your public opinion polls hovering in the basement. What's next? Stay the course.

Author and Fortune 500 consultant Dr. Peter Hirsch offers helpful advice:

> Your thoughts determine your feelings, and the emotional energy of feelings is a powerful ally...The instant you succeed in turning a negative to a positive, that negative is going to do its best to reassert itself. After all, it's fighting for its life! But then, so are you—and it is really all up to you which of the two wins. [2]

In reality, not all expectations can be met. We are living in real time, with real-time setbacks and sidetracks. At times, the winds of modern culture can change quicker than you can adjust the sails. Political and economic dangers often loom beneath the surface like sharks with a sweet tooth. The skilled leader will learn to navigate rough seas by...

> consulting the maps,
> watching the weather,
> avoiding dangers, and
> making midcourse adjustments.

Here are some important questions to ask yourself when evaluating expectations:

- *How realistic is my primary objective or goal?* Does it have natural explosives built in? Does it really reflect the will of stakeholders?

- *What real or imagined fear am I fighting?* Whom will I disappoint if this vision, cause, or objective is not successful?

- *Is this expectation realistic?* Have I set or borrowed an achievement standard that doesn't reflect personal or corporate resources? Am I reaching farther than my funding or staffing?

Expectations are moving targets, not fixed. They are situational rather than static. If you don't meet a personal expectation, you have not failed—you have simply been thrust into a creative environment where new ideas are born from adjustment and new goals rise from the ashes.

> *Coming together is a beginning,*
> *staying together is progress, and*
> *working together is success.*
>
> **JAMES B. MILLER**

## Personal Agendas

I enjoy watching people unpack their belongings when they arrive for a business meeting. The items have changed over the years. Once they included a spiral-ring notebook, daily planner, and Cross pen—pulled from a leather attaché case. Now they may include a tablet, laptop, and smartphone—pulled from an over-the-shoulder designer bag. But regardless of the storage systems, everyone is carrying a personal agenda. The published agenda is always just one of many agendas.

This reminds me of the school board in one town that proposed adding a new chandelier to the principal's office. As soon as the proposal was put to a debate, one of the board members—an elderly man with a hearing problem—angrily stood to his feet and spoke against the project. "I just want to go on record as being totally against this waste of taxpayer money!" he said, pounding his fist on the table for added emphasis.

The board member's reaction came as a surprise to the other members. This was the first time their colleague had responded in such a negative and vehement way. After a long period of silence, the board chairman politely asked why adding the chandelier would be wasteful.

Again the board member stood and took a resolute stance, "Look, the principal only lives a couple of miles from the school. If the teachers can drive themselves to work, so can he. In my opinion he doesn't need a paid chandelier to drive him to the office."

Mistaking "chandelier" for "chauffeur," the gentleman evidently needed a new Energizer battery for his hearing aid—and hadn't gotten many of the Word Power questions right in his *Reader's Digest*! But the story gives a bit of insight into what leaders might face when personal agendas sneak into meeting agendas.

How to deal with personal agendas?

- *Politely*. Honey is a better solution than vinegar. Effective leaders coat their responses with respect. Kindness is a solvent that soothes friction.

- *Objectively*. What can you learn from the purportedly better idea? Sometimes there *is* a better way to build the mousetrap!

- *Tactfully*. By asking leading questions, you might discover an improved compromise—a solution that will add productivity without dividing people.

- *Firmly.* When all else fails, play the traffic cop and give directions in a firm but respectful way.

## Focus

Peter Hirsch gave the analogy of a master archer who was teaching his students archery technique. As they prepared to shoot at a distant target, the teacher stopped them and asked what they saw. One described the sky and the landscape around the target. The master told him not to shoot and to put his bow down. The other student said he saw a bulls-eye at the center of the target.

The master archer gave the command to shoot, and that student's arrow flew through the air to the center of the target. Hirsch said the difference between the two students was a single-minded focus.[3]

### 4 Common Leadership Mistakes

1. Hiring too quickly.
2. Expecting too much.
3. Assuming you're right.
4. Failure to delegate.[4]

Multitasking may be the mantra of the new millennium. If we can't be everywhere at once, we'll use FaceTime. If we can't do everything at once, we'll use robotics. We have more arrows flying at once than ever before, but our consistency at hitting the bull's-eye is still subpar.

Maybe it's time for an archery lesson: Develop single-minded focus. Here are some ways to bring focus to your leadership.

*1. Avoid "distraction zones."* Obviously there are some environments that detract rather than direct. You know them well. It could be the TV room or computer room at your house, or it may be the break room at the office. You know the distraction dangers that lurk in those places, so avoid them when leadership duties call.

*2. Reward yourself.* Focus should have an added value. Give it one. When you complete all or part of a project, take a break. It may include food or a round of golf or a shopping trip. Whatever the reward, make sure your mind knows you've reached a "focus milestone."

*3. Put your whole self into the focus.* Focus your inner self—your disciplined thinking. Spend time away from the noise and the clutter to mull over the direction or decision.

Focus your outer self—your interests and observations of the culture around you. Watch and listen for workable solutions and note them.

Focus your social self—the ideas and advice of your trusted friends and associates. Learn to leave the authority badge at home and take a friend to lunch just to gain from his or her knowledge or experience.

The challenges aren't the champions. You are...when you determine to overcome them with your own best practices or the best practices of others.

In the next chapter, you'll read about one of the government's classic gaffes.

Chapter 8

# Effective Team Communications

*Great leaders make sure everyone around*
*them knows what's going on.*

George Hathaway tells the story of a communications snafu during J. Edgar Hoover's tenure as director of the FBI. Intrigued by his agents' sudden focus on the Canadian and Mexican borders of the United States, the director made an inquiry and discovered the problem.

Weeks before, Hoover had dictated a memo to his field offices. Wanting to be sure it was correct, his secretary asked him to look at the communique before sending it out. Scanning the page layout of the memo, he saw that the borders were uneven and made a notation to his secretary: "Watch the borders."

The secretary saw the note and concluded that Mr. Hoover's comment was a special directive, so she inserted it in the copy. The sudden intelligence activity along the borders was simply a broken link in the communications chain.[1]

---

*Effective team communications is a*
*twenty-first-century necessity.*

---

Effective team communications is a top-tier concern. Professional sports lead the field when it comes to team communications. From microphones in football helmets to instant replay in baseball to race cars with satellite receivers, the days of holding up signboards to communicate would seem to be as obsolete as the last deviled egg at the end of a company picnic.

And yet if you look closely, you'll still see coaches and team leaders using old-fashioned hand signals to communicate from the sidelines. Offensive coordinators who call plays through their headsets hide their mouths with cardboard play charts to keep the opponent's staff from reading their lips. The bottom line is to get the message to team members as effectively as possible.

Without effective communication methods and policies, people managers aren't coaching from the sidelines—they're spectating from the stands! Effective team communications is a twenty-first-century necessity.

What are some barriers to team communication, and how can you overcome them?

## Communication Breakdown

The earliest days of the West African Ebola crisis were characterized by a breakdown in communications in the hospital where a victim was treated. Of course, the media had its usual glut of reporting, but the lessons went far beyond the headlines. Somewhere in the system, a glitch prevented the message of danger from getting to the medical team.

You may have experienced similar crises, though not on such an international level. But any breakdown in organizational communications can be dangerous—and contagious. Where does it start?

- Someone doesn't take ownership of the communications.

- Communication policies aren't observed.

- Immediacy turns into complacency.

- Communication methods are obsolete.

- Important messages lack clarity.

Let's break those down and examine possible solutions to overcome communications barriers.

### When You Should Delegate and When You Shouldn't

1. Keep the project when it must be done a specific way. Delegate if there is more than one right way.

2. Keep the project when it takes longer to explain than to complete. Delegate if it's a skill the employee needs to learn.

**3.** Keep the project when you really enjoy it.
Delegate if it's no longer in your job description.[2]

**Ownership.** When no one is in charge, everyone is—and that's an incubator for chaos.

The leader is the chief messenger. Some messaging can't be delegated. For example, any changes in policy, staff, or brand should come from the top. The messages will be carefully examined and proofed for accuracy or relevance by executive-level personnel, but they should be owned by the CEO.

**Policies.** What is the communications policy of your organization? You may use a basic *who*, *what*, *when*, and *how* process. For example, Paul Argenti and Janis Forman suggest these components for a communications plan in times of crisis:

- Referring media relations to a central location. *Who* speaks for the organization?

- Notifying employees ahead of media releases. *When* should appropriate details be released—and to whom?

- Designating a crisis communications headquarters. *How* should information be released?

- Creating an official description of management's plan and logistics. *What* is the key message of releases?[3]

**Complacency.** Communication can break down quickly. An urgent situation not addressed with immediacy can turn to complacency. And complacency is like an untreated wound that becomes infected. Ignoring a situation won't make it go away. Even if it ducks out of sight, it will reemerge with energized fury at a later time.

If a major breakdown occurs, your immediate response is of utmost importance. Let me unpack an acrostic that might help you patch the communication lines.

**I***nvestigate the situation thoroughly.*
   What failed? What was the effect?

**M***eet with the leadership team.*
   Gather ideas for remedying the situation.

**M***ap an action plan.*
   What should be the response,
   and when should it begin?

**E***stablish a line of communication.*
   Reach out to those affected.

**D***etermine the response tool.*
   What communication method will be used?

**I***nstruct team members.*
   Use the situation as a learning tool.

**A***ssess collateral damages.*
   What is the wider range of affect?

**T** *ake responsibility for the breakdown.*
    Apologize appropriately.

**E** *valuate the response.*
    How has the situation improved?

**Communication methods.** Breakdowns are ideal times to evaluate your communication methods. These days, *how* you communicate is almost as important as *what* you communicate. If you're locked into the paper trail as your main method, you might be due for an upgrade, though a note or letter will never lose its luster. Realistically, we live in the instant-access age. The first line of communication is usually electronic.

E-mail has replaced the business letter in most cases. Its roominess allows for a longer message, and it can be delivered almost instantaneously. It can also be used in conjunction with a more formal follow-up letter.

### Five Tips for Connecting with a Remote Team

1. Create a regular schedule and stick with it. Avoid the temptation to have impromptu meetings with those who are under your roof.

2. Incorporate rituals into your virtual meetings, such as quickly sharing "highs and lows" since

your last meeting to get warmed up and create a window into your team's world.

3. Ask for input from those who are remote first, and then canvass the in-person team members. Avoid falling into the "out of sight, out of mind" syndrome.

4. Send all documents in advance so everyone is literally on the same page.

5. Consider having everyone attend electronically if your team is only partially remote to level the playing field.[4]

In some cases, the business letter is still the gold standard. It is more personal, more businesslike, and more secure than e-mail, and it is unlikely to be misrouted or read by the wrong parties.

**Clarity.** All communication formats—including social media—have their inherent strengths, weaknesses, and risks. But none is effective without a clear and concise message. As a rule of thumb, communications should be proofed at least three times—once for spelling and grammar, another time for clarity, and a third time for overall impression.

## Team Conflict

Mike Myatt wrote in *Forbes* magazine, "Leadership is a full-contact sport, and if you cannot or will not address conflict in a healthy, productive fashion, you should not be in a leadership role."[5] Conflict is a fact of organizational life. A leader is, among many other things, a referee. It's his or her job to bring calm to the chaos.

> *High performance expectations are consistently the best predictors of team success.*
>
> **CLAY CARR**

Organizations are people-filled and people-driven. Unfortunately, those people don't always get along. Charlie Brown's classic quote is apropos: "I love mankind, it's people I can't stand!" Sometimes skilled team members feel threatened or offended, and they fire off words that can never be retrieved. A leader's task is to get the team back on track. Myatt suggests these keys for dealing with conflict:

- *Define acceptable behavior.* Publish a "delegation of authority" statement.

- *Hit conflict head-on.* Seek out areas of potential conflict and proactively intervene.

- *Understand the "What's in it for me?" factor.* Make note of others' motivations.

- *Pay attention to the importance factor.* If the issue is important enough for conflict, it is important enough to resolve.

- *View conflict as opportunity.* Divergent positions can stimulate innovation.[6]

Effective leadership brings calm to the chaos and affirms the actors without condoning their actions.

- Deal with communication issues on a personal level, not corporate.

- Make sure team members know you want to hear their side of the story.

- Use tough love to assure them that the conflict must be settled for the team to function properly.

## Pointless Meetings

Meetings for meetings' sake are boring and unproductive. Effective communications take the mundane out of meetings. For leaders, meetings are as common as brushing their teeth— and just as necessary. Many managerial "toothaches" can be prevented with preliminary meetings of the minds and nego- tiated plans of action. Let the members of your team be the first to know of policy or schedule changes, and invite them to provide their input. When your team is left out in the cold, you can be sure relationships will turn icy.

The frequency of meetings is optional, but their regularity

creates a comfort zone for your team. Meetings are not more productive because of their frequency; they are more productive because they are planned that way. Here are four key ingredients of a productive meeting.

*A definite purpose.* That begins with you, the leader. If you are able to clearly define the purpose of the meeting, your team will be more apt to see it as an opportunity rather than an obligation. You could give a one-sentence purpose statement in your meeting invitation. For example, "Our Wednesday meeting will include staffing the new design department."

*A planned agenda.* Written or not, you need to know which topics will be on the table. A written agenda for regularly scheduled meetings is a must. It is the map that leads participants to a common destination.

*A firm schedule.* By setting start and end times, you provide your team with a sense of urgency and prevent conversational side trips. You also provide boundaries for those who tend to lunge at every opportunity to give their extended opinion.

*A consistent focus.* As chair of the meeting, you have the obligation to keep it on track. Sometimes that will include a kindly interruption. "That's a good idea, Sheila—let's put that on next week's agenda." Kindness and courtesy are never out of order.

You are the guide who leads meeting participants to peaks of victory and through valleys of discouragement. Lead cheerfully, confidently, and purposefully. Give time for input without being critical or defensive. And always remember to close the conversation with affirmation.

## Lack of Accountability

Amway cofounder Rich DeVos tells of a friend who gives a Trust Medal to his children when they reach the age of 21. They are accountable to earn the medal, however. Their receiving it depends on such things as their relationships with the family, good personal behavior, and community service. Their twenty-first birthday party becomes the occasion when their accountability is honored with the medal and a celebration.[7]

A breakdown in communication is also a breakdown in accountability. One or more persons have failed to meet their obligations to others. Palm trees don't grow in Alaska—it's too cold there. Tropical plants need warmth. Orchids don't bloom in the desert—it's too dry. Delicate flowers need plenty of moisture. If you want any plant to grow, you must provide the right atmosphere.

Obvious?

Not always. Many leaders try to grow a team without providing the right climate. Team members need affirmation and accountability in order to thrive. Starve them for recognition or lower your expectations for their behavior, and they'll dry up faster than a tiger lily in Tunisia. But give them plenty of encouragement for doing the right thing, and they'll grow strong as sequoias and multiply like zucchinis. Actually, affirmation and accountability are inevitably linked.

Here's how to create an atmosphere of accountability and affirmation for your team.

**Celebrate success.** You've been pushing for weeks on a big project. Team members exhausted themselves, but the big push paid off. Your big day came off without a hitch. Now it's over, right? Not quite. As a leader, you have one more job to do. Celebrate this success with the team.

Never let an achievement slip by unnoticed. When minor objectives are reached, call attention to them in staff meetings or write e-mails of praise. When major goals are accomplished, hold a party for the team, take the staff to dinner, or issue a bonus. When your team succeeds, have a celebration. They will feel affirmed, and they will learn that accountability has a payoff.

**Praise in private.** Set an example of affirmation and accountability by encouraging team members one-to-one. Make lavish use of cards, e-mails, or phone calls that say "I appreciate you." Hearing "Way to go!" will encourage your volunteers and set the standard for encouragement. Soon, you'll notice staff members doing the same with their teammates—and with you!

**Praise in public.** Praise team members for their completions and victories in front of each other. Let all team members know that their peers are making valuable contributions. Show them that they should praise their teammates' success. Mention achievements at staff meetings. Affirm a teammate in the hearing of others. Be fair and evenhanded, avoid playing favorites, and beware of arousing envy. Simply let each team member know you appreciate the contribution of the others.

**Pay attention to team needs and progress.** Your praise will ring hollow if it's not grounded in reality. "You're doing a great job" will be meaningless to a team member who knows her contribution was subpar.

Keep connected. Observe your team members' achievements and failures, and offer encouragement accordingly. Asking, "How can we learn together from this setback?" can be just as affirming as praising a success.

**Treat your paid staff like volunteers.** They really are! Every one of them could be working somewhere else. They work with you because they believe in what the team is doing—and they believe in you. Give them positive reinforcement. Tell them that their work matters. Let them know you appreciate the way they take responsibility for their work. They'll work harder, and you'll look smarter.

I like the story of the elderly couple sitting on a porch swing on a warm summer evening. The husband suddenly speaks up. "Thelma, I'm proud of you."

"What?"

"I'm proud of you," the husband repeats.

"What did you say? You know I can't hear anything without my hearing aid!"

He takes a deep breath and speaks louder. "I'M PROUD OF YOU!"

She stands up and says, "WELL, I'M TIRED OF YOU TOO!"

Effective communication in any relationship or organization is a challenge. But challenges can be overcome.

In the next chapter I'll show you how to build winning relationships.

## Chapter 9

# Building Winning Relationships

*Leaders know how important it is to reinforce
the team effort with honest recognition, but
they don't hand out bouquets of plastic roses.*

What do you need to be a leader? People who will follow you.

The simplicity of the premise is almost mind-blowing. But take away the people component, and you're left with a stack of job descriptions, empty offices, a pile of certificates, and a useless copy of a vision plan.

---

*If you're a leader, you're in
the people business.*

---

Paper and brick don't relate—they're only useful in the hands of real people. If you're a leader, you're in the people business.

"Practical skills are only one of four dimensions of leadership," Dan Reiland wrote. "There is also a spiritual dimension, a psychological dimension, and an organizational dimension. And all four components build on a foundation of relationship."[1]

Leadership is not a one-size-fits-all practice. People are almost incomprehensibly diverse. You can be heading in the same general direction as another, but you may not be on a parallel path.

Author Alan C. Fox underscores that: "In every human interaction, you can't assume that the other person is just like you. Each of us has to learn to recognize, respect, and hopefully enjoy our differences...Though we all live on the same planet, we cannot walk precisely in each other's footsteps."[2]

## A Case Study

Stacy was obviously a great hire. She had a warm personality, a quick wit, excellent computer skills, and a great telephone presence. Seeing her at her administrative secretary desk before any of the other staff had arrived in the morning, the HR manager knew he had hit the hiring jackpot. Her supervisor agreed. She proved time and again that her stellar résumé was not a fluke.

Her performance continued to excel, but something began to change. Her supervisor noticed she didn't have the exuberance that marked her personality at the beginning. Sometimes her colleagues asked her if she was feeling all right. They began wondering aloud if something was troubling her.

One day there was a turnaround. Her supervisor needed someone to write a blog for the department, and he mentioned it to Stacy. "I'd be glad to give that a try!" she said excitedly. She knocked the first blog out of the park! Stacy was a great writer, and she had design skills as well. Within the week, she had come up with a brand for the communication piece—including a fresh new logo and banner. Other department heads asked her supervisor if he had outsourced the blog. "No," he responded. "I just found someone in-house who isn't just a doer—she's also a dreamer."

Stacy had been on the office's production team all along, but she was in the wrong role.

Building relationships must be at the top of the leader's priority list. And key to understanding the building *process* is to understand the building *materials*—people. And understanding people includes putting them in the right role.

## The Production Crew

Consider for a moment the way team members are like a theatrical production crew. There are at least six key roles: writer, producer, director, technical director, stage manager, and actor. Understanding their typical responsibilities and skills may give you insights on team assignments and expectations.

*Writer.* The writer is the visionary member of the production team. His or her job is to give form to an idea or theory. That task may be assigned, or it may be original. Either way, the talent of the visionary is the foundation for the actions of the entire crew. Put that person in a director's position, and they might fail terribly. Like Stacy, they aren't drivers, they're dreamers. You may not have the budget for another hire, but you can get the best from your visionary by adding the communication responsibilities to his or her job description.

*Producer.* In a theatrical production team, the producer is the fine-strokes person. They put tracks under the writer's ideas. They gather the resources, delegate set design, hire the actors, raise funds, and direct advertising. Does that description bring someone in your office to mind? That's the person you can trust to work out the details on time and under budget. They may be a terrible writer. They thrive on doing rather than dreaming.

*Director.* Directors answer only to ownership. They determine the atmosphere. They stage. They rehearse the actors. They evaluate performance and make adjustments for the next performance. Getting them to be a producer would be painful. They are broad-strokes people who take the details and put them on display. In the office setting, they are the department heads or managers.

*Technical director.* Technical directors keep the lights on. Whether directing the sound crew, supervising equipment maintenance, setting the lights, or hiring crew, they are the go-to persons. Give them a tool belt or an advisor's cap, and their presence will be large on the set. The person in your office with the technical skills holds the same large presence—especially when the computers fail, the air conditioning quits, or the phone system goes on the fritz. Their job is to keep the equipment running. It may be one of the easiest fits in your human resources repertoire. Tie a technical director to a writer's or director's desk, and they may blow a fuse!

*Stage manager.* The stage manager is the director's liaison on the set. Running rehearsals, cueing actors, or making logistical decisions, the stage manager makes sure everyone is in their designated place during rehearsal and performance. In the office setting, a stage manager is the supervisor or team leader, guiding daily operations according to the director's instructions.

*Actor.* Actors may be last on the list, but they are of first-tier importance. They interpret and implement contributions up and down the organizational ladder. They are pivotal to the success of the production. They may be the caboose in the leader-staff train, but in their case, the caboose actually gives motion to the train. Their success depends on both skill and the ability to follow directions. And like workers in your office staff, their performance also hinges on the information and affirmation they receive from their leaders.

In a theatrical production, the success of the performance rests on the interaction between the production crew members. It's the same in any organization. When the relationship-building stops, the performance flops.

## The Beatitudes of Interpersonal Relationships

Be gracious—give honor to whom honor is due.
Be positive—make people feel good about being around you.

Be courteous—don't forget the magic words.
Be truthful—never hedge the facts.
Be kind—do unto others…
Be aware—look for ways you can be of service.
Be thankful—don't make people search for your
    appreciation.

## Building Relationships in Context

This is the age of avatars—assumed identities communicating and contracting with other assumed identities. But the real action is personal and in real life. This real-life context includes *online* communications, but it is not limited to them. It also includes interactions based on *shared lifestyle, family relationships, support services, helpful skills,* and *network development.* Relational proficiency in those contexts is the mark of effective leadership.

**Relationships happen in the context of shared lifestyle.** Relationships are born in the communities of life. They may form at work, at school, at church, or in neighborhood interactions. Your path crosses another's, and you discover common interests, common networks, common values, and common ethical behaviors.

In that context, you engage in conversations that might result in a planned meeting. And in that meeting environment, you give and take opinions that provide the glue for a continuing life conversation.

Leaders build relationships by implementing a similar strategy. They find common ground, start conversations in a safe environment, and learn how to give and take opinions for the sake of strengthening the relationship.

**Relationships happen in the context of family.** You've heard the expression "We're one big, happy family." Immediately, two things come to mind. First, big (or small) families are not always "one." They may assemble in one place, but that doesn't guarantee they are one. Oneness comes from buying in to a common interest.

Second, families are not always happy. I have two brothers for whom I would die. I consider them my best friends. We spent a major part of our lives living under the same roof, but we didn't always agree, and we weren't always happy. That's the DNA of family—together but sometimes separate.

When we were young, we had different ideas about what we should do, where we should go, and when, but that didn't keep us from being one. As we grew older, we expanded our families, chose our career paths, and developed new interests. Sometimes our paths were very different—even in ideologies—but we were still brothers at heart. Family isn't static; it moves in different directions, but the members share a common mission.

Leaders understand the importance of building relationships with family dynamics in mind. Families don't have to agree on everything. Family members have unique personalities that often don't blend. But in the end, they usually work out their differences—as long as they are open to dialogue and willing to compromise for the common good.

**Relationships happen in the context of support services.** You may not think of the cable repairman as part of your team, but he or she really is. The repairman has skills that are beyond your expertise. From the minute that person walks through the door with a bag of tools, you have expectations of a remedy. You're not intimidated by their expertise. You're not jealous that they drive a company vehicle. You're interested in their use of the right skills and tools to fix a problem.

**Relationships happen in the context of helpful skills.** Unique skills add depth to the team. Leaders work with those who make things work. For example, a quarterback can't win a football game alone. He needs specialists who block, run, catch, tackle, and so on. The quarterback doesn't want to be a fullback—he just wants to hand off the ball to the fullback. The quarterback doesn't want to play defense—he just wants to depend on the defenders to gain field advantage. Any quarterback worth his bonus just wants to be the best quarterback he can be.

Build relationships by affirming the skills of team members.

- Let them know you trust their uniqueness.
- Treat them as experts.

- Provide further training for them.
- Provide tools for their work.

**Relationships happen in the context of network development.** Network building is a four-lane highway, not a one-way street. You build relationships to build networks to build relationships to build networks. Any return on those investments is a bonus, not a given. Your career contacts and professional network are by-products of your friendship-building, and you build friendships intentionally.

- You use people's names when conversing with them.
- You express gratitude for their helpfulness.
- You are immediately available to them when needed.
- You remember their key events and special days.
- You are supportive and not critical of them.
- You are available to help their extended family.
- You constantly seek their betterment.

Your work is the "net" in "network." When you make an effort to put your comfort on hold in order to bring ease to others, you draw them to you.

*Leadership is the stewardship of the people
(the work environment) that a person oversees
to successfully guide the team toward the
larger purpose for which the team works.*

PETER BLOCK

**Relationships happen in the context of social media.**
Social media offers leaders instant access for building relationships. A tweet or post is a modern nod, smile, or handshake to colleagues or peers. When used wisely, it can do in seconds what would normally take hours. But like anything, social media can be overused and abused. Here are some things to consider before posting.

- Is the message professionally relevant or beneficial?

- Will the recipient consider a forwarded message spam?

- Has the message been double-checked for accuracy, grammar, and spelling?

- Is the forwarded message from a proven and reliable source?

- Does the message criticize another colleague or organization?

- Does the message include a personal greeting?

- Does the message encourage interaction and response?

- Will the message simply take up time or space for the recipient?

- How does the message bring encouragement or help to the recipient?

- Is the message concise rather than wordy?

---

### Ten Rules for Relationships

1. Always speak first.

2. Be observant.

3. Be generous.

4. Remember names.

5. Recognize potential.

6. Forget mistakes.

7. Listen more than you talk.

8. Be the first to apologize.

9. Acknowledge your mistakes.

10. Laugh easily.[3]

## Nine Laws of Relational Leadership

Do you want to build relationships that strengthen your team and motivate them to five-star excellence? Of course you do! Consider these nine important laws that drive that kind of relational leadership.

*1. Always seek the welfare of others.* You are the team's *provider*. Your task is to provide the emotional, financial, physical, and spiritual resources team members need to excel. You offer a safe and supportive environment where they can grow in their character, skillfulness, career, and relationships without fear of reprisal or harm.

*2. Always listen to understand others' comments.* You are the team's *friend*. Your task is to listen intentionally and intently to your team members. Some may express criticism, evaluation, suggestions, or complaints. In each case, provide a safe place for them to express themselves. You don't have to agree with everything they say; just express your friendship and personal concern by listening with your ears, your eyes, your mind, and your heart.

*3. Always reward others for completing tasks.* You are the team's *judge*. Your task is to reward the efforts of team members with visible and audible approval. The reward may be a monetary gift, a special privilege, or a handwritten or electronic note, but it is always accompanied by a genuine expression of gratitude for a completed task.

*4. Always expect the best practices of others.* You are the team's *coach*. Your task is to gain the best from each team member by expecting their best. Affirm their unique abilities, encourage their progress, and teach them how to meet and overcome personal and professional challenges.

*5. Always express gratitude for others' work.* You are the team's *model*. Your task is to set the standard of courteous and thoughtful behavior by being courteous and thoughtful. Enthusiastically praise team members for their kindnesses to you, and in so doing, provide a marker for their expressions to others.

*6. Always look for the motive behind others' behavior.* You are the team's *counselor*. Your task is to view team members' rebellious or antisocial behavior as an outward expression of an inner emotional or spiritual conflict. Express your concern with a readiness to listen and with opportunities for treatment, including referral. Refuse to accept unproductive or disruptive behavior as a personal attack. Rather, see it as an opportunity to pursue healing.

*7. Always provide information vital to others' work.* You are the team's *communicator*. Your task is to provide an appropriate and direct line of information to team members about the mission and methods of your organization—including personnel or policy changes.

*8. Always increase others' skills.* You are the team's *trainer*. Your task is to build the professional and personal strengths of team members through continuing education—formally or on the job. Consider each team member as a future leader, and do everything in your power to improve their skill set.

*9. Always take responsibility for others' work environment.* You are the team's *cheerleader*. Your task is to provide a positive and productive daily atmosphere. Set the tone of the day by your enthusiasm and friendliness. Speak positively of others and encourage social times with the team to foster friendships and understanding.

A rookie real estate agent met with her sales manager to report a problem. "I know you taught us to be resourceful and to think on our feet, but I have a situation that really has me baffled."

"Let's talk about it," her manager replied.

The rookie explained the situation. "I sold a young couple ten acres of property for their future home, and now three of those acres are covered in water. Evidently it used to be a swamp."

Her manager gave her a stern look. "Angie, I'll have to say I'm a bit disappointed. You're one of our best salespersons. Tell them you forgot to mention there was lake frontage, and sell them a kayak!"

Interpersonal relationships are challenging at best, but the solution certainly isn't discouragement and deceit—it's honesty and affirmation.

When it comes to working with people, great leaders know how to turn negatives into positives. That's what the next chapter is all about.

## Chapter 10

# Leadership That Transforms

*The best leaders are those who can inspire others
to reach for something greater than themselves.*

A kindergartner burst through the front door of his house. He tossed his backpack in one direction and his lunch in another. His mother took it all in, and as most mothers would, she imagined the worst. "Scotty, did you have a problem at school today?"

The little boy beamed with enthusiasm, "No, Mom! I had an awesome day!"

Relieved that he hadn't eaten someone else's lunch or spent any time at the police headquarters, she said, "Well, let's hear about it!"

"Mom, I learned how to measure the distance on a road map! Isn't that totally awesome?"

Mom replied, "It totally is! Now what are you going to do with all that learning?"

The boy paused to think about the question and then answered, "I got it! The next time we take a vacation, I'll read the map and tell you the how-fars!"

Then his voice level lowered, and he said, "Mom, don't worry, I'll still need you to tell me the where-tos."

Effective leadership is more than learning the how-fars. It also includes knowing the where-tos and supporting others on the journey. Effective leaders help others to...

- feel better about themselves,
- be more established in their value system,
- have more confidence in their skills,
- be more confident in the leadership of others,
- be more confident in their own leadership, and
- feel more comfortable in their interpersonal relationships.

In other words, it *transforms* them.

According to the Wikipedia article "Transformational Leadership," this model was introduced by James Mac-Gregor Burns, and it "inspires followers to change expectations, perceptions, and motivations to work towards common goals...based on the leader's personality, traits and ability to make change through example, articulation of an energizing vision and challenging goals." Bernard M. Bass expanded on Burns's original ideas, defining transformational leadership in terms of the "impact that it has on followers."

Business blogger Pearl Zhu gives additional insight into transformational leadership:

"Trans" is derived from Latin and as a prefix means "across, on the far side, and beyond." "Trans" connotes a bridging characteristic, thus, transformational leaders practice forward-looking, future-connecting thought leadership. They facilitate a redefinition of a people's mission and vision, a renewal of their commitment and the restructuring of their systems for goal accomplishment.[1]

Burns provides his own definition of the transformational leadership model:

Such leadership occurs when one or more persons engage with others in such a way that leaders and followers raise one another to higher levels of motivation and morality…it raises the level of human conduct and ethical aspirations of both leader and led, and thus has a transforming effect on both.[2]

## Transformational Leaders…

- *Develop the vision*. They transform the organizations and head them down new tracks.
- *Grow more leaders*. They develop a relationship of

mutual stimulation and elevation that converts
followers into leaders.

- *Promote changes.* They inspire others to follow a
  vision.

- *Build trust.* They engender trust, admiration, loyalty, and respect among their followers.

- *Drive mind shift.* They engage with followers as
  whole people, rather than simply as employees.
  Their mindset is based on self-reflective changing
  of values and beliefs.[3]

In 40-plus years of leadership responsibilities as an admin-
istrator and an instructor, I have practiced transformational
leadership. When I began, it didn't have the brand, but as it
evolved, I continued to incorporate its principles in my leading and teaching. As I continue to learn about it in principle,
I have observed some defining characteristics.

---

*People want to be recognized for who
they are and what they've done.*

---

## It Leads with Gratitude

Rich DeVos lists "thank you" as one of the ten most powerful phrases. He recounts that at the completion of their world
headquarters building, Amway held an open house that was

separate from its dedication event. Every skilled worker who was involved in the construction of the building was invited. DeVos said those invited included...

> the men and women who drew the blueprints, erected the steel girders, placed the brick, installed the windows, built the roof, laid the carpet, and hung the drapes. The founders and executives wanted the workers to see the results of their hard work. They stood in line to shake the hands of the workers, have a brief conversation with them, and say a personal "Thank you"...

> People like to be thanked and they *need* to be thanked! The well of kindness can dry up when we fail to acknowledge the givers of gifts.[4]

I think that's a very important model for every leader. The faithfulness of team members in putting the finishing touches on an organization's mission should not be overlooked. Specifically, gratitude should be given...

**By expressions of appreciation.** Obviously, a verbal thank-you is the go-to expression—and yet it's often overlooked. You may have been on the receiving end of the grand oversight. You worked long hours and made personal and family sacrifices to complete a project—and didn't receive a solitary word of appreciation. You didn't know it at the time, but you were enrolled in Leadership 101.

You express your appreciation in your own unique way, but you should always include a verbal expression. Appreciation motivates work.

> Researchers at the Wharton School at the University of Pennsylvania randomly divided university fund-raisers into two groups. One group made phone calls to solicit alumni donations in the same way they always had. The second group—assigned to work on a different day—received a pep talk from the director of annual giving, who told the fund-raisers she was grateful for their efforts. During the following week, the university employees who heard her message of gratitude made 50% more fund-raising calls than those who did not.[5]

**By expressions of affirmation.** DeVos says another top-ten powerful phrase is "I'm proud of you." "Behind a lot of hard work is a simple desire to be recognized as the best in our profession, to be given a more impressive job title, to win an award or see our name in the paper. Everyone appreciates a pat on the back."[6]

When I was a boy in Sunday school, students were rewarded for such things as perfect attendance or memorizing

Bible verses. The prizes were so small, they would bring a chuckle today—a pencil, a bookmark, or a glow-in-the-dark plastic statuette. They would hardly be worth mentioning in today's economy, but when my name was called and I was invited to the platform to pick up the award, I felt as if I were receiving an Olympic medal. It wasn't the cost or the size of the award that mattered—it was the recognition that I had excelled.

Today's reward in a similar situation might be a coupon for a fast-food sandwich or a 50 percent discount to a theme park, but the principle is the same. People want to be recognized for who they are and what they've done. They want affirmation and even crave it. Transformational leaders know that. They know that by affirming their team members, they might even be filling a void that some have felt since childhood.

**By expressions of acceptance.** How do you know when you're on the inside track? Usually when someone trusts you with insider information. "I trust you" is another of DeVos's ten most important phrases. When we trust someone, we are freer to keep them informed about the things that matter most to them. Transformational leaders are not information hogs. They are open about the important stuff. Team members need information to do their work. They also need it to feel accepted in the organization.

Transformational leaders always treat their team members like insiders. They openly share items not deemed confidential for reasons of security. They understand the team should be first to know when the organization changes navigation. They know that information is a symbol of security.

## 20 Ways to Say "Thank You"

1. Send a card or e-mail that says, "I'm glad you're part of the team!"

2. Remember birthdays and anniversaries.

3. Give a mini-perk, such as free tickets to the zoo, free car-wash coupons, or a gift certificate to a favorite restaurant.

4. Meet for lunch (on you) and ask, "How can I support your work?"

5. Sandwich corrective comments between two compliments.

6. Make a one-to-one contact by phone, e-mail, or in person at least once a month.

7. Send a card or e-mail that says, "Thanks for the great job on this project."

8. Thank staff members for doing things that are part of their job description.

9. Take time to highlight achievements at every staff meeting.

10. Give a staff member a free day off after completing a big project.

11. Treat the team to lunch once in a while.

12. Praise your team members to your superiors, and let your team know about what you said.

13. Give regular performance evaluations even when there are no problems, and use them as opportunities to offer affirmation.

14. Ask a staff member for an opinion on something that's not in his or her area of responsibility.

15. Inquire about staff members' family life and health.

16. Send a card or e-mail that says, "I respect your skills."

17. Use your annual report to celebrate team successes, not merely report numbers.

18. Ask, "How can I pray for you this week?" and then be faithful to pray about the needs.

19. Throw a party for staff and spouses to celebrate the achievement of yearlong goals.

20. In a one-on-one setting, say, "Your contribution has eternal value because…"

## It Leads with Resolve

A book I cowrote with Air Force Brigadier General Robert Redwine, *Minute Motivators for the Military*, recounts the story of a World War II slogan that has survived a century. "Keep calm and carry on" was printed on posters distributed to British citizens prior to the war. Its message of perseverance was intended to warn them to prepare for the anticipated airstrikes and yet to resolve to go on with their lives. [7]

The slogan fits transformational leaders. They push forward despite threats or obstacles. They refuse to live under the clouds of pessimism and doubt when the sun is shining only a day or project completion away. They stay focused even in the blurring times.

David Allen, author of the bestselling *Getting Things Done* and consultant for many Fortune 500 companies, says we are all born with "a mind that wanders every chance it gets. And one of the places it wanders to most is the to-do lists of our life...While some of that wandering is healthy and useful, much of it is distracting and stress-producing, draining our energy and reducing our ability to stay focused, creative and productive." [8]

This little anonymous poem wraps it all together.

> It takes a little courage and
> a little self-control
> And a grim determination,
> if you want to reach the goal.
> It takes a deal of striving and a firm
> and stern-set chin,

No matter what the battle,
if you really want to win.
There's no easy path to glory,
there's no easy road to fame.
Life, however we may view it,
is no simple parlor game.
But its prizes call for fighting,
for endurance and for grit,
For a rugged disposition,
and a don't-know-when-to-quit.

## It Leads with Servanthood

Transformational leadership is not self-seeking. It longs to serve others. "Rather than looking out only for their own interests, great leaders learn to ask win-win questions like these: What can I do for you? What can we do together? How can this benefit both of us? Learn to ask, How can I help others to succeed? and you will succeed as well. A leader who is always looking for credit will soon be a solo performer."[9] What does transformational leadership look like under the hood?

*Its work ethic is people-focused.* Whatever transformational leaders do, they always have the welfare of people in mind. Whether the mission is a service or a product, they seek to improve the lives of others.

*Its lifestyle choices are humanitarian.* Transformational leaders choose their causes carefully, but they usually reflect the conscience of their community. They have an open heart to the needs of others and are wisely generous in their support for relief efforts.

*Its interrelationships are solid.* Transformational leaders take their associations seriously. They are faithful to their friends and family. They value their colleagues. They interact with their peers. They listen to others and learn from them. They can be depended on. Malcolm S. Forbes said, "You can easily judge the character of a man by how he treats those who can do nothing for him."

*Its transactions are honest.* Transformational leaders make agreements on the premise of integrity. They keep their word. They deliver on their promises. They meet their end of the bargain. Transparency characterizes their life. They live above the line morally and financially.

> *Greatness is not about personality; it is about humility plus will. That is where the essence of leadership begins.*
>
> **JIM COLLINS**

## It Leads with Excellence

Success is not a zero-sum game. Excellent leaders know that their achievement does not depend on someone else's failure. There is more than enough success to go around. The most effective leaders are not afraid to help others reach their goals. They believe in the power of the win-win situation.

Zig Ziglar often said that you can get everything you want if you help enough others get what they want. In order to do that, you'll have to have an attitude of openness. That may require a change of mind.

No team will follow a truly selfish leader. The team may establish a good work regimen and perform well, but unless the members respect their leader, the team will not excel.

The best leaders display that seldom-seen virtue of humility. They discover real worth in their ability to generate team excellence, not personal recognition. Here are five marks of greatness in a leader.

*Excellent leaders don't care who gets the credit as long as the job gets done.* Actions take precedence over accolades. Goals are more important than gold. Ribbons are incidental to right behavior. Excellent leaders don't draw attention to themselves—they express appreciation for the contributions of others.

*Excellent leaders are willing to put the mission ahead of their personal agenda.* They've discovered the greater joy of giving their lives for something worthwhile. The purpose, mission, and objectives of the organization are paramount, while the personality and personal achievement of the leader are secondary.

*Excellent leaders are quick to forgive.* Little people hold grudges; big people forgive and forget. Little people nurse insults and look for revenge; big people let bygones be bygones. All great leaders are big people. They earn respect but never demand it. They avoid petty squabbles and develop thick skin.

*Excellent leaders delight in the achievements of others.* Excellent leaders realize they themselves can never accomplish all they dream; others must carry out their vision. So they invest in others, encourage them, train them, and enable them to succeed. The best leaders realize there's plenty of success to go around, and they help those around them succeed.

*Excellent leaders give credit where it's due.* They know they are highly skilled, yet they realize that their success depends on the contribution of others. They know there are no "little people" in the organization—every person's contribution is significant. Excellent leaders know how to say, "Well done!" and they say it often.

Enjoying great success does not depend on having a great ego. In fact, the opposite is almost always true. Those who think the most of themselves are usually respected little by others.

Former Georgia governor and businessman Sonny Perdue said, "My philosophy of leadership is to surround myself with good people who have ability, judgment, and knowledge, but above all, a passion for service." I agree.

# Notes

**Introduction**

1. Associated Press, "Runaway Train Travels 70 Miles, *Cincinnati Post*, May 16, 2001, www.highbeam.com/doc/1G1-74627572.html.

2. Nancy Armour, "Becky Hammon on being Spurs assistant coach: 'Why couldn't I be the first?'" *USA Today*, August 11, 2014, www.usatoday.com/story/sports/nba/2014/08/11/becky-hammon-san-antonio-spurs-assistant-coach-wnba/13931299/.

**Chapter 1—Defining Your Vision**

1. Allyson Willoughby, "How to Create a Workplace People Love Coming To," *Leadership Now*, www.fastcompany.com/3028368/bottom-line/how-to-create-a-workplace-people-love-coming-to.

2. Cited in Lindsay Lavine, "How Greyhound Is Trying to Stay Relevant at 100 Years Old," *Fast Company*, June 5, 2014, www.fastcompany.com/3031415/hit-the-ground-running/how-greyhound-is-trying-to-stay-relevant-at-100-years-old.

3. Willoughby, "How to Create a Workplace People Love Coming To."

4. Dale Galloway, "The Incredible Power of Vision," in *Leading with Vision*, ed. Dale Galloway (Kansas City: Beacon Hill Press, 1999), p. 13.

5. Cited in William Safire and Leonard Safire, eds., *Leadership: A Treasury of Quotations for Everybody Who Aspires to Succeed as a Leader* (New York: Simon and Schuster, 1990), p. 240.

6. Pat Williams with Jim Denney, *Coach Wooden: The 7 Principles that Shaped His Life and Will Change Yours* (Grand Rapids: Revell, 2011), p. 26.

7. Meghan M. Biro, "Leadership Is About Emotion," *Forbes*, December 15, 2013, www.forbes.com/sites/meghanbiro/2013/12/15/leadership-is-about -emotion/.

8. Cited in Safire and Safire, *Leadership*, p. 22.

9. Cited in Paul Lee Tan, *Encyclopedia of 7700 Illustrations*, (Rockville, MD: Assurance, 1979).

**Chapter 2—Developing a Vision Plan**

1. Stan Toler, *Stan Toler's Practical Guide to Leading Staff: How to Empower Your Team and Multiply Ministry* (Indianapolis: Wesleyan Publishing House, 2012), p. 53.

2. John Swartz, "Michael Dell beat Icahn, now he's reinventing PC stalwart," *USA Today*, June 10, 2014, www.usatoday.com/story/tech/2014/06/ 09/michael-dell-rare-interview-pc-consolidation-battle-with-carl-icahn /9914017/.

3. Paul Argenti and Janis Forman, *The Power of Corporate Communications: Crafting the Voice and Image of Your Business* (New York: McGraw-Hill, 2002), p. 71.

4. David L. McKenna, *The Leader's Legacy* (Newburgh: Barclay Press, 2006), p. 21.

5. Max De Pree, *Leadership Is an Art* (New York: Doubleday, 1989), p. 11.

6. Margaret Starbuck, "Women Leading in a New Era," *Gifted for Leadership*, December 2013, www.giftedforleadership.com/2013/12/women_leading_ in_a_new_era.html.

7. Williams, *Coach Wooden*, p. 79.

8. Cited in Donna Faulkner, *Mandela* (New Word City, 2014), n.p.

9. John C. Maxwell, *The Right to Lead: Learning Leadership Through Character and Courage* (Nashville: Thomas Nelson, 2010), p. 41.

10. Jim Collins and Morten T. Hansen, *Great by Choice* (New York: Harper Business, 2011), p. 182.

11. Cited in Benjamin Franklin Tefft, *Life of Daniel Webster* (Philadelphia: Porter and Coates, 1854), p. 394.

## Chapter 3: Casting a Vision

1. Nicole Fallon, "14 Leaders Share Best Leadership Advice," *Business News Daily*, November 30, 2013, www.businessnewsdaily.com/5541-best-leadership -advice.html.

2. Mary Jo Asmus, "5 Ways to Notice Hidden Leadership Talent," *Aspire Collaborative Services*, June 25, 2014, www.aspire-cs.com/5-ways-to-notice -hidden-leadership-talent.

3. Work Group for Community Health and Development, University of Kansas, "Conducting Needs Assessment Surveys," *Community Tool Box*, chapter 3: Assessing Community Needs and Resources, section 7: Conducting Needs Assessment Surveys, ctb.ku.edu/en/table-of-contents/assessment/assessing -community-needs-and-resources/conducting-needs-assessment-surveys/ main.

4. Ibid.

5. Mark A. Smith and Larry M. Lindsay, *Leading Change in Your World* (Marion: Triangle Publishing, 2001), pp. 160-61.

6. Kevin Cope, *Seeing the Big Picture: Business Acumen to Build Your Credibility, Career, and Company* (Austin: Greenleaf Book Group Press, 2012), p. 93.

## Chapter 4—Quality Testing a Vision

1. Jack Stahl, *Lessons on Leadership: The 7 Fundamental Management Skills for Leaders at All Levels* (New York: Kaplan Publishing, 2007), pp. 10-11.

2. *Chick-fil-A*, "Our Giving Tradition," www.chick-fil-a.com/Company/ Responsibility-Giving-Tradition.

3. Chuck Salter, "Chick-fil-A's Recipe for Customer Service," *Fast Company*, www.fastcompany.com/resources/customer/chickfila.html.

4. Kerry Hannon, "Sheryl Sandberg's 5 Best 'Lean In' Tips For Women," *Forbes*, March 13, 2013, www.forbes.com/sites/nextavenue/2013/03/13/sheryl -sandbergs-5-best-lean-in-tips-for-women/.

5. Argenti and Forman, *The Power of Corporate Communications*, p. 74.

6. Jeffrey L. Cruikshank, *The Apple Way: 12 Management Lessons from the World's Most Innovative Company* (New York: McGraw Hill, 2006), p. 176.

7. Cited in Fallon, "14 Leaders Share Best Leadership Advice."

8. Georgea Kovanis, "Millennials shape the new holiday shopping experience," *Detroit Free Press*, November 23, 2014, www.freep.com/story/life/shopping/georgea-kovanis/2014/11/23/millennials-shape-new-holiday-shopping-experience/19414121/.

9. McKenna, *The Leader's Legacy*, p. 61.

10. Ibid., p. 72.

## Chapter 5: Vision Skills

1. Stan Toler, *Minute Motivators for Men* (Oklahoma City: Dust Jacket Press, 2011), p. 137.

2. George Hathaway, *Leadership Secrets from the Corporate Office* (New York: MJF Books, 2009), pp. v-vi.

3. Michael Hyatt, *Platform: Get Noticed in a Noisy World* (Nashville: Thomas Nelson, 2012), p. 6.

4. Stan Toler, *The Inspirational Speaker's Sourcebook* (Kansas City: Beacon Hill Press, 2009), p. 32.

5. Granville N. Toogood, *The Articulate Executive* (New York: McGraw-Hill, 1996), p. 189.

6. Harry M. Jansen Kraemer Jr., *From Values to Action: The Four Principles of Values-Based Leadership* (San Francisco: Jossey-Bass, 2011), pp. 173-74.

7. Gina Hernez-Broome and Richard L. Hughes, "Leadership Development: Past, Present, and Future," *Center for Creative Leadership*, www.ccl.org/leadership/pdf/research/cclLeadershipDevelopment.pdf.

8. Cited in Kevin Kope, *Seeing the Big Picture: Business Acumen to Build Your Credibility, Career, and Company* (Austin: Greenleaf Book Group Press, 2012), p. 78.

### Chapter 6: Coaching Objectives

1. Associated Press, "Michigan 14-year-old Completes 40 Mile Trek While Carrying Brother on Back," *Fox News,* June 9, 2014, www.foxnews.com/us/2014/06/09/michigan-14-year-old-completes-40-mile-trek-while-carrying-brother-on-back/.

2. Kaylee Heck, "Michigan Teen Carries His Brother for 57 Miles on His Back for Cerebral Palsy Awareness," *ABC News*, June 8, 2015, abcnews .go.com/US/michigan-teen-carries-brother-57-miles-back-cerebral/ story?id=31615343.

3. Stahl, *Lessons on Leadership*, p. 64.

4. Hathaway, *Leadership Secrets from the Corporate Office*, p. 13.

5. Ron McClung, "Positive Perspective," *Wesleyan Publishing House*, January 31, 2014, www.facebook.com/wesleyanpublishinghouse/posts/696983547 020500.

6. Cited in Shandra Martinez, "Rich DeVos: Family Assembly Created to Teach Grandchildren About Wealth," *M Live Media Group*, April 1, 2014, www.mlive.com/business/west-michigan/index.ssf/2014/04/rich_devos_ family_assembly_cre.html#incart_river_default.

7. Hathaway, *Leadership Secrets from the Corporate Office*, p. v.

8. Josh Bersin, "Spending on Corporate Training Soars: Employee Capabilities Now a Priority," *Forbes*, February 4, 2014, www.forbes.com/sites /joshbersin/2014/02/04/the-recovery-arrives-corporate-training-spend -skyrockets/.

9. Dave Ramsey, "7 Life Lessons from Truett Cathy," Dave Ramsey (blog), www.daveramsey.com/blog/7-life-lessons-from-truett-cathy.

10. Stan Toler, *ReThink Your Life* (Indianapolis: Wesleyan Publishing House, 2008), p. 34.

11. Stan Toler and Keith Hawk, *Terrific! Five Star Customer Service: Learning About Excellent Service from Special People* (Oklahoma City: DustJacket Press, 2013), p. 3.

12. Ibid.

## Chapter 7: Overcoming Leadership Challenges

1. Michael Hyatt, "The Top-10 Characteristics of Lousy Leaders," Michael Hyatt (blog), michaelhyatt.com/lousy-leaders.html.

2. Peter Hirsch, *Success by Design: 10 Biblical Secrets to Help You Achieve Your God-Given Potential* (Minneapolis: Bethany House, 2002), p. 78.

3. Ibid., p. 108.

4. Nicole Fallon, "4 Common Leadership Mistakes (And How to Avoid Them)," *Business News Daily*, September 25, 2013, www.businessnewsdaily.com/517 4-avoiding-leadership-mistakes.html.

## Chapter 8: Effective Team Communications

1. Hirsch, *Success by Design*, p. vii.

2. Sara McCord, "When You Should Delegate, and When You Shouldn't," http://mashable.com/2014/07/23/delegating-work/.

3. Argenti and Forman, *The Power of Corporate Communications*, pp. 260-61.

4. Lee Colan, "11 Techniques for Connecting With Your Remote Team," *Inc.*, www.inc.com/lee-colan/11-techniques-for-connecting-with-your-rem ote-team.html#ixzz3B3SLYnID.

5. Mike Myatt, "5 Keys of Dealing with Workplace Conflict," *Forbes*, February 22, 2012, www.forbes.com/sites/mikemyatt/2012/02/22/5-keys-to-dea ling-with-workplace-conflict/.

6. Ibid.

7. Rich DeVos, *Ten Powerful Phrases for Positive People* (New York: Center Street, 2008), p. 117.

## Chapter 9: Building Winning Relationships

1. Dan Reiland, *Amplified Leadership: 5 Practices to Establish Influence, Build People, and Impact Others for a Lifetime* (Lake Mary: Charisma House, 2011), p. xxiii.

2. Alan C. Fox, *People Tools: 54 Strategies for Building Relationships, Creating Joy, and Embracing Prosperity* (New York: Select Books, 2014), p. 101.

3. Stan Toler, *If Only I Could Relate to the People I'm Related To* (Kansas City: Beacon Hill Press, 2010), n.p.

## Chapter 10: Leadership That Transforms

1. Pearl Zhu, *Digital Master: Debunk the Myths of Enterprise Digital Maturity* (Lulu Publishing Services, 2015), p. 80.

2. James MacGregor Burns, "Transactional and Transformational Leadership," chap. 19 in *The Leader's Companion*, ed. J. Thomas Wren (New York: Simon and Schuster, 1995), p. 101.

3. Zhu, *Digital Master*, pp. 80-81.

4. DeVos, *Ten Powerful Phrases for Positive People*, pp. 88, 92.

5. Harvard Medical School, "In Praise of Gratitude," November 1, 2011, www.health.harvard.edu/newsletter_article/in-praise-of-gratitude.

6. DeVos, *Ten Powerful Phrases for Positive People,* p. 73.

7. Stan Toler and Robert Redwine, *Minute Motivators for the Military* (Kansas City: Beacon Hill Press, 2014), p. 47.

8. David Allen, *Making It All Work* (New York: Penguin Group, 2008), p. 37.

9. Stan Toler, *Stan Toler's Practical Guide for Pastoral Ministry* (Indianapolis: Wesleyan Publishing House, 2007), p. 173.

## About the Author

Stan Toler is a dynamic international speaker, having spoken in more than 90 countries. He has written more than 100 books, including his bestsellers *The Secret Blend, The Relational Leader, The Exceptional Leader, The Inspirational Speaker's Resource, ReThink Your Life, Total Quality Life, Terrific! Five Star Customer Service,* and his popular Minute Motivators series. His books have sold more than three million copies.

For many years, Toler served as vice president of John C. Maxwell's INJOY Leadership Institute, teaching seminars and training church and corporate leaders to make a difference in the world.

**Dr. Stan Toler**
PO Box 720230
Oklahoma City, OK 73172-0230
Web: www.stantoler.com
E-mail: stan@stantoler.com

To learn more about Harvest House books and
to read sample chapters, visit our website:

**www.harvesthousepublishers.com**

HARVEST HOUSE PUBLISHERS
EUGENE, OREGON